TRUE TO LIF

ELEMENTARY

Joanne Collie
Stephen Slater

CLASS BOOK

CAMBRIDGE
UNIVERSITY PRESS

PUBLISHED BY THE PRESS SYNDICATE OF THE UNIVERSITY OF CAMBRIDGE
The Pitt Building, Trumpington Street, Cambridge, United Kingdom

CAMBRIDGE UNIVERSITY PRESS
The Edinburgh Building, Cambridge CB2 2RU, UK
40 West 20th Street, New York, NY 10011–4211, USA
477 Williamstown Road, Port Melbourne, VIC 3207, Australia
Ruiz de Alarcón 13, 28014 Madrid, Spain
Dock House, The Waterfront, Cape Town 8001, South Africa

http://www.cambridge.org

First published 1995
Ninth printing 2001

Printed in the United Kingdom at the University Press, Cambridge

ISBN 0 521 42140 3 Class Book
ISBN 0 521 42141 1 Personal Study Workbook
ISBN 0 521 42142 X Teacher's Book
ISBN 0 521 42143 8 Class Cassette Set
ISBN 0 521 42144 6 Personal Study Cassette
ISBN 0 521 48574 6 Personal Study Audio CD

CONTENTS

COURSE OVERVIEW

Unit	Language focus	Vocabulary	Topics	Review
1 FINDING OUT	*to be* *there is, there are* articles: *a, an, any* adjectives, sentence structures	names, addresses, jobs buildings and facilities	meeting people giving directions inside a building important things in life learning languages	instruction words expressions of location
2 WHAT HAVE YOU GOT?	*has got / have got* *some (some/any)* subject pronouns and possessive adjectives contractions	families and countries personal possessions homes and furniture	asking about family asking about homes and possessions	dates, months, years Unit 1
3 WHAT WOULD YOU LIKE TO EAT?	present simple question forms the verb *to have* *would like* and *I'd like* countable and uncountable nouns	food and meals prices	breakfast food room service ways of memorising names prices in different cultures	Unit 1 Unit 2
4 A SENSE OF COLOUR	question forms with present simple verbs present simple verbs in positive sentences: 1st / 3rd person	clothing, colour time expressions: *never, once a year, twice a year*	uniforms buying clothes cultural meaning of colours producing a blue rose	Unit 2 Unit 3
5 GOOD HABITS, NEW ROUTINES?	present simple verbs: positive, negative, questions frequency adverbs	daily routines habits and customs	morning people language learning habits national customs queues	Unit 3 Unit 4
6 THE WAY YOU LOOK	expressing opinions agreeing and disagreeing *I'd like* for wishes adjectives and modifiers *too* and *not enough*	appearance: face and body describing personality	deducing personality from the face important qualities in friends personal ads	Unit 4 Unit 5
7 WHAT CAN WE DO?	*can* for ability, skills or permission *can* and *could* for requests past simple of *to be* and *to have* *could* as past tense of *can*	personal skills and abilities childhood	special skills ages at which things are allowed in different countries thinking about the past	Unit 5 Unit 6
8 LOVE IT OR HATE IT!	verb (*like/dislike*) + noun verb + *-ing* form	good and bad features of cities, countries and jobs pets	talking about likes and dislikes describing cities and countries national characteristics compared	Unit 6 Unit 7
9 THOSE WERE THE DAYS	revising past tense of *to be, to have, to go* past simple tense: regular verbs object pronouns	memories of schooldays and the past	remembering school days and friends remembering past addresses phones with screens	Unit 7 Unit 8
10 ONCE UPON A TIME	past simple: irregular verbs	stories and storytelling books, films, TV programmes	creating a narrative an African storyteller preferences in films, books and TV	Unit 8 Unit 9
11 WHAT'S GOING ON?	present continuous for things happening now, temporary or developing situations contrast present simple and present continuous	daily routines and happenings the quality of life	contrasting everyday life and holidays changes in the cost of living	Unit 9 Unit 10
12 MAKING PLANS	present continuous: future events, already arranged *going to* + infinitive: future events, already arranged / things you intend to do	work or recreational activities language learning activities	weekend plans a company's weekly diary resolutions for learning	Unit 10 Unit 11

Unit	Language focus	Vocabulary	Topics	Review
13 BETTER AND BETTER	comparative and superlative adjectives	features of countries facilities in cities	comparing countries of the world Istanbul and Brasilia a list for visitors to your city	Unit 11 Unit 12
14 A SPIRIT OF ADVENTURE	present perfect with *ever* or *never* for unfinished time with *this week/month/year* contrast present perfect with simple past	sporting activities illness stress and relaxation learning English	experiences with dangerous sports fitness reflexology a progress report on learning English	Unit 12 Unit 13
15 DOES BEING TIDY SAVE TIME?	*-ing* forms	everyday activities offices, storing information computers	personal aspects of tidiness and forgetfulness dealing with paper in offices ways of managing information	Unit 13 Unit 14
16 OUR NEIGHBOUR-HOOD	relative pronouns present perfect with *just* and *yet* giving directions: imperatives	neighbourhoods direction expressions	drawing maps of neighbourhoods comparing neighbourhoods in different countries changes in neighbourhoods	Unit 14 Unit 15
17 IT'S WORTH DOING WELL	adverbs ending in *ly* contrasting adjectives/adverbs connecting words of sequence imperatives	hobbies and crafts rude/polite actions	how people do things talking about hobbies contrasting cultural views of politeness a modern etiquette book	Unit 15 Unit 16
18 ON YOUR TRAVELS	recommendation/advice: *should, shouldn't* obligation: *has to / have to* lack of obligation: *doesn't/don't have to*	travel, tourism	remembering past journeys advice for air travellers advice for tourists to your country travelling in Kashmir, Turkey or Japan good and bad tourists	Unit 16 Unit 17
19 A LOOK AT LIFE!	expressing wishes with *would like*: all forms *would* with other verbs	views on life beauty	sayings about life how people spend time wishes in life comparing cultural views of beauty	Unit 17 Unit 18
20 I'M SO SORRY!	apologising complaining	shops and shopping situations hotel situations	experiences in shops behaviour in different cultures formal and informal apologies	Unit 18 Unit 19
21 ALL YOU NEED IS LOVE ... OR MONEY	verbs *need/want* + noun or infinitive *don't need / don't want* + noun or infinitive	money needs, success in life	advice to young people attitudes to money the life of a stockbroker comparing needs and wants comparing ideas of success	Unit 19 Unit 20
22 THE RIGHT CLIMATE?	*what's it like* questions *if* clauses + imperatives or present simple	weather, climate protection against the weather	describing summer or winter temperatures imagining an ideal day natural disasters and emergencies	Unit 20 Unit 21
23 CELEBRATIONS	offering, inviting accepting, declining *shall* for offers	national festivals family celebrations	comparing national festivals Kwanzaa, a new festival talking about personal celebrations a good host in St Lucia and India	Unit 21 Unit 22
24 LOOKING AHEAD	the present simple for talking about the future the future simple for future facts and predictions	age and attitudes to age personal predictions about the future predictions about the future of the world	talking about personal plans media bias against older people ways of predicting the future views about the future of the planet	Unit 22 Unit 23

FINDING OUT

Language focus:
to be: positive, negative, question forms
there is, there are
articles: *a, an, any*
adjectives; sentence structures

Vocabulary:
names, addresses, jobs
buildings and facilities

A

1 Excuse me, what's your name?

asking and giving names, addresses, telephone numbers

Make a list of people in your class. Ask questions and write down the answers.

– What's your name?
– What's your address?
– What's your telephone number?

HELP

Is that your full name?
Is that your family name?
Is that your first name?
How do you spell that?

ENGLISH CLASS

NAME	ADDRESS	TELEPHONE
Pilar Sánchez	Calle Mayor, 28 Salamanca Spain	66 24 81

2 He's a waiter. What do you do? | vocabulary and articles; question forms

a restaurant   an office   a van   a school   a surgery   a garage

Match the jobs with the right buildings – or the van.

a secretary   a waiter   a waitress   a teacher   a doctor   a dentist   an accountant
a lawyer   an electrician   a plumber   a mechanic   a businessman   a businesswoman

What do you do? Mime to others in the class.
Others in the class: ask questions.

Example: A: *Are you a waiter?*
B: *Yes, I am. (No, I'm not.)*

HELP

I'm a parent.
I'm unemployed.
I'm a housewife.
I'm retired.

3 Where are you from? | listening; speaking

📖 Listen to four people meeting.
Match the names and the countries.

Yaprak   Arturo   Helga   Kenji

Answer the questions.

Example: A: *Is Yaprak from England?*
B: *No, she isn't. She's from Turkey.*

– Is Arturo from Mexico?
– Is Helga from the United States?
– Is Kenji from China?

Mexico   Japan

Work with a partner. Find out about each other.

Example: A: *Where are you from?*   B: *I'm from Lisbon.*
A: *Are you a businesswoman?*   B: ....
A: *Are you a parent?*   B: ....

Denmark

HELP

Are you part-time?
Are you full-time?

Turkey

QC Now do the **Quick Check** exercises your teacher will give you.

1 Where are you now? | listening |

⊂⊃ Listen to the recording. Where is the first person? Where is the second person? Put a tick (✓) in the table.

	in a classroom	in an office	at home
Person 1	......	......	......
Person 2	......	......	......

What about you? Where are you now? Think of a friend. Where's your friend now? With a partner, ask and answer questions.

Example: A: *Where's your friend now?*
B: *She's (He's) at home / at work / in India.*
A: *What's her (his) name? Where's she (he) from?*

2 In the room, there's a carpet | *there's (there is), there are*; vocabulary and writing |

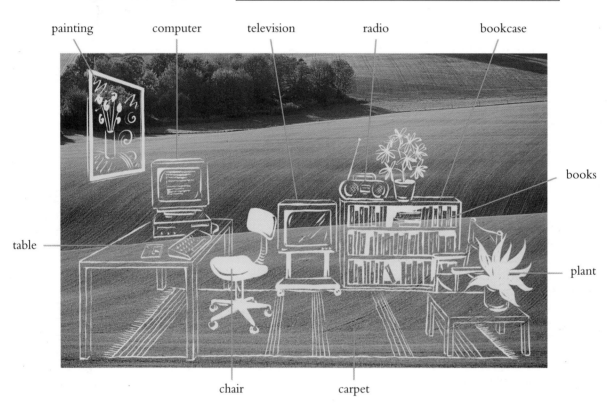

painting   computer   television   radio   bookcase

table

books

plant

chair   carpet

⊂⊃ Listen to a description of the room in the picture. There are two things wrong with the description. What are they?

There isn't a .... There aren't any ....

With a partner, talk about the room you are in. Take turns.

Example: A: *In the room there's a light.*   B: *There's a carpet.*
A: *There are chairs and tables.*

Write a description of the room you are in – but with one thing wrong. Read your description to others. What's wrong?

Example: A: *There are chairs and tables. There's a light, a radio and a carpet.*
B: *Where's the radio? There isn't a radio.*

3 Is there a lift in the building?

question forms; short answers

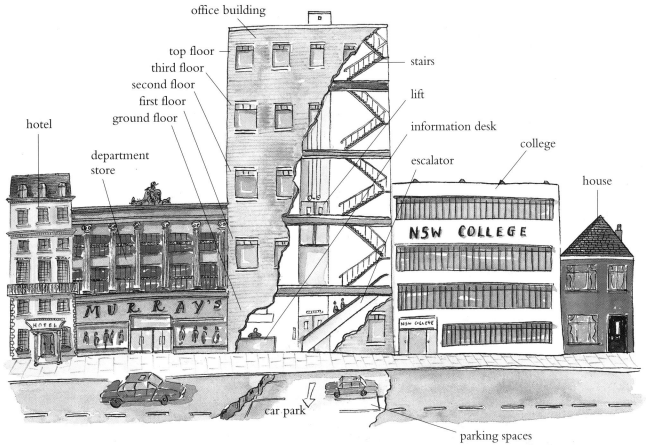

Ask and answer questions about the building you are in.

Example: A: *Is there a lift in the building?*   B: *Yes, there is. (No, there isn't.)*
          B: *Are there any parking spaces?*   A: *Yes, there are. (No, there aren't.)*

Choose a building in your town or city. What is it? (a hotel, an office building,
a school, etc.) Does the building have a name?

Listen and answer the questions about your building. Ask a partner the same
questions about their building. What is it? Can you guess?

4 How good is your memory?

review of *a, an, any* and vocabulary

Study the example.

Example: *Is there ^a carpet?*

Write in the missing words in the sentences.

– Are there escalators?
– Is there lift?
– Are there public telephones?
– Are there parking spaces?
– Is there information desk?

Close the book. What can you remember? Write down words under these headings:

Things in rooms   *Things in buildings*

Key
A list of 5 things: your memory is good.
A list of 10 things: your memory is very good.
More? Your memory is excellent!

QC Now do the **Quick Check** exercises your teacher will give you.

1 The important things in a good workplace   vocabulary; adjectives

plants

nice people

phones

computers

no smoking

comfortable chairs

natural light

a coffee shop

parking spaces

Add your own ....

What are the important things in a good workplace? Choose three. Write them down.

Work in groups. Talk about your choices.

Example: A: *I think the important things are nice people, a coffee shop and plants. What about you?*
B: *Nice people, natural light and parking spaces.*

2 The important things in life   reading; subject–verb–adjective

Simple maths? Choose one of these.

Money = happiness   = ☺

Money + a happy family = happiness
Money + an interesting job = happiness
An interesting job + free time = happiness
.... + ... = happiness
(write your own)

Work in groups. Talk about your choices.

Example: A: *For me, money is happiness. What about you?*
B: *No, for me money isn't important.*
Happiness is a happy family and free time.

Read the text. How many jobs are there in it?

Say if this is true or false in the text:

the key thing = the important thing = the main thing

Read the text again. What is important for the four people?

Petra: ....   Ben: ....

Luisa: ....   Zoran: ....

What's important for you? Compare your ideas with a partner.

Example: A: *I think Petra's right. The key thing for me is my children. What about you?*
B: *Well, the main thing for me is free time, not money.*

Money is happiness
– Is that true?

For unemployed people, money is all important. But for people with good jobs, money is not always the key thing. Other things are just as important.

Take these four typical people. Is money the main thing for them? Petra, a nurse, says, 'The key thing in my life is the happiness of my children.' Ben is an engineer, and for him, learning new things at work is the main thing. Luisa is a waitress. She says, 'The nice thing about my job is meeting new people – it's not really the money.' Zoran is a part-time teacher. Having a lot of free time is important to his happiness.

Economists say people work to get more money. Is that true for you? No? Then say this to your company: 'Give me an interesting job, a lot of free time with my family, and you can keep part of my salary!'

3 What about learning a new language? What's important? | speaking |

Look at the examples then complete your pie chart for learning English.

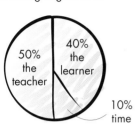

Compare your charts in groups and talk about them.

Example: A: *For me, learning English is 40 per cent ...., 50 per cent .... and 10 per cent .... What about you?*

B: *For me, it's 90 per cent .... and 10 per cent ....*

QC Now do the **Quick Check** exercises your teacher will give you.

PERSONAL STUDY WORKBOOK

In your Personal Study Workbook you will find more exercises to help you with your learning. For Unit 1, these include:

- numbers and prepositions
- *there is* and *there are*
- vocabulary of jobs and countries
- visual dictionary – buildings and their facilities

D REVIEW AND DEVELOPMENT

PART 1

1 Language for the English class | instructions to you, the learner |

Here are some instruction words. Match the words and the pictures. Ask other learners – then ask the teacher.

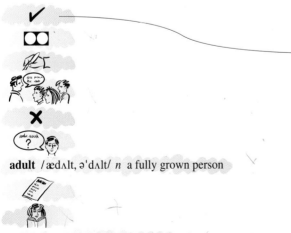

Tick
Put a cross
Read
Listen
Write
Guess
Work in pairs
Tell the class
Use a dictionary
Make a list
Complete the sentence

These instruction sentences are all in this unit of the book. Look back at the unit and complete the sentences.

1. Compare your .... in groups.
2. Put a tick ....
3. .... with a partner.
4. Read .... description to ....
5. Ask .... and write down ....

Compare your answers in groups. Make sure you understand the instructions. Find other instruction sentences in Unit 1. Make a list.

Example: *Take turns.* (page 8)

2 What does *salary* mean? | questions; listening |

Here are some questions for the English class.

1. What does .... mean?
2. How do you spell it?
3. Could you speak more slowly, please?
4. Could you repeat that, please?
5. Could you write that on the board, please?
6. How do you say .... in English?

☐☐ Listen to two people asking questions. Look at the list of questions above. Tick the questions you hear.

One question is not in the list. Write it down:

....

PART 2

1 Where's the computer room? It's next to the lift. | reviewing expressions of location; listening |

With a partner, read these sentences.
One sentence is not correct. Which one?

The reception desk is opposite Room 1.
Room A is next to Room B.
Room C is next to the lift.
Room C is opposite Room B.
Room D is opposite Room C.
The lift is at the end of the corridor.

☐☐ Listen to three people asking the way in this building. Write down the missing rooms on the plan.

1. Where's the computer room on the plan?
   Write CR (*computer room*) on the plan.
2. Where's the library on the plan?
   Write L (*library*) on the plan.

Choose two:

public telephones   a coffee shop
a restaurant   a clock   stairs

Put them in different parts of the building.
With a partner, ask questions and answer them.

Example: A: *Where's the coffee shop?*
          B: *It's on the second floor, at the end of the corridor, on the left. (There isn't a coffee shop.)*
          B: *Where are the public telephones?*
          A: *They're next to the lift. (There aren't any.)*

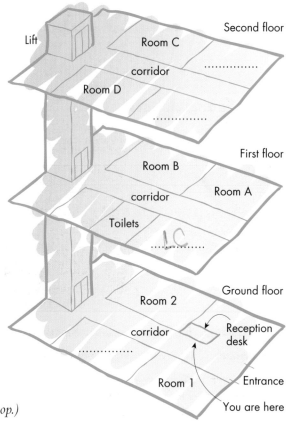

2

WHAT HAVE YOU GOT?

Language focus:
has got / have got
some (some/any)
subject pronouns and possessive adjectives
contractions

Vocabulary:
families and countries
homes and possessions

A

1 He's got two daughters   *have got / has got*; vocabulary; discussion

A

My ....
My mother
My grandmother
My baby brother
My ....
Me

B

C

D

E

Look at the paintings. Fill in the missing words.

Read the sentences. Choose the right person in the paintings.

She's got a little sister and a brother. Who is she?
He's got two daughters. He hasn't got a wife. Who is he?
She's got two granddaughters and a grandson. Who is she?
'We've got a son and a daughter.' Who are they?
He's got one daughter. Who is he?

2 Have you got any friends in other countries?

Have you got ...? questions with short answers

▭▭ Answer the questions on the recording.

	1	2	3	4	5
Yes. (✓)	......	......	......	......	......
No. (✓)	......	......	......	......	......

Now move around the class and ask people questions.

Example: A: *Have you got any brothers or sisters in another country/city?*
B: *Yes, I have. / No, I haven't.*

Make notes. How many people have got family or friends in another country?

3 He's got a cousin in Rio de Janeiro   writing a short paragraph

Write a few sentences about someone in the class.

Example: *Maria's parents and grandparents are in her country, Spain. She hasn't got any daughters or sons, but she's got a sister in another city, a brother in New Zealand and a cousin in Thailand. She's got some friends in Canada and a pen friend in Scotland – in Edinburgh.*

Read the sentences – but don't say the name. Can others guess who it is?

QC Now do the **Quick Check** exercises your teacher will give you.

B

1 He's got some money   vocabulary: possessions

a mirror   1 .... a comb   a calculator   2 .... a handkerchief

a credit card   3 .... house keys   a portable computer   4 ....

With a partner, match
the pictures and the words.   a pen   money   car keys   a mobile phone

Guess. What do you think? What has the woman in the picture got in her handbag? What has the man got in his briefcase?

I think she's got: ....

I think he's got: ....

🎧 Listen and check your guesses. Some things in the picture are not on the recording. What are they?

The ...., the .... and the .... are not on the recording.

Compare your answers in groups.

2 Have you got any car keys? | have got; some and any |

With a partner, list three things you've got with you today.

Example: *We've got a bag and a pen and some money.*

Join another pair. Ask questions and answer them.

Example: PAIR A: *Have you got a calculator?*
PAIR B: *Yes, we have. / No, we haven't.*
PAIR B: *Have you got any money?*
PAIR A: *Yes, we have. / No, we haven't.*

3 How many plants have you got? | vocabulary |

Fill in the first column of the questionnaire about you. Write *0, 1, 2, 3, 4, 5* or *lots*.

How many ...	have you got?	has Peter got?	has Sheila got?
phones	......	......	......
radios	......	......	......
plants	......	......	......
beds	......	......	......
books	......	......	......

🎧 Now listen to the recording. Fill in the second and third columns about Peter and Sheila.

4 Has she got a phone in the bathroom? | listening |

Write *Yes, I have* or *No, I haven't* in the first column. Then listen to the recording and write *Yes, he/she has* or *No, he/she hasn't* for Peter and Sheila.

	You	Peter	Sheila
Have you got …			
a phone in the bathroom?	....	....	....
a television in the bedroom?	....	....	....
any plants in the kitchen?	....	....	....
any beds in the sitting room?	....	....	....

Check your answers with a partner. Now ask questions and note the answers.

Example: A: *How many books have you got?*   B: *I've got lots.* or *I haven't got any.*

Find a new partner. Report the answers to your questions.

Example: *Juan has got lots of books. He hasn't got any plants. He hasn't got a phone in the bathroom.*

QC Now do the **Quick Check** exercises your teacher will give you.

C

1 It's got a nice little kitchen | *it's got*; reading and discussion |

Read the letter.

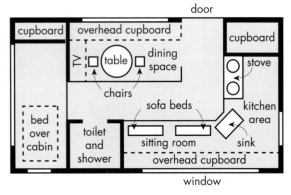

What has the motorhome got? With a partner, make two lists under these headings:

It's got   *It hasn't got*

a shower   a bath

Compare your lists with other students.

Are motorhomes popular in your country? Are they good for long holidays? Are they good for two people or for families?

Tucson, 5th May

Dear Greta,
Well, here we are in Arizona. This is a picture of our motorhome! It's not very big but it's got a big bed over the driver's cabin for Sev and me, and two little beds in the sitting room for the children. The beds are our sofas during the day, and we've got a tiny dining space with a table and some chairs. There's a nice little kitchen with a stove and some cupboards, and we've even got some plants, over the sink. There isn't a bath, but we've got a good shower – and a toilet of course. It's almost like home! Now for Texas! See you in July.
Lots of love from
Julie, Sev, Lucy, James

2 My bedroom's my favourite room | vocabulary |

Choose your favourite room in your house: the kitchen, the bedroom, the sitting room, the bathroom. What have you got in the room? Make a list of things. Use a dictionary or ask the teacher if you need help.

old things	*new things*	*small things*	*big things*
....	....	....	....
....	....	....	....
....	....	....	....

Make a plan of your favourite room. Show what is in it. Tell a partner about it.

Example: *My favourite room is the* ....

        It's .... (big; small)

        It's got .... (tables; chairs; beds; lamps)

        They're .... (old; new; big; small)

QC Now do the **Quick Check** exercises your teacher will give you.

PERSONAL STUDY WORKBOOK

- vocabulary of family relationships, rooms and furnishings in homes
- pronunciation work
- *have got*
- reading and writing letters
- visual dictionary – possessions

D   REVIEW AND DEVELOPMENT

REVIEW OF DATES, MONTHS, YEARS

1 When's your birthday? | listening; vocabulary; conversation |

CD Listen to three people: Sam, Alex and Penny. Mark their birthdays on the chart. Mark your birthday on the chart.

Now ask three other students.

Example: A: *When's your birthday?*

    B: *It's **in*** .... (month)

       *It's **on** the* .... (date)

       of .... (month)

Mark all your birthdays on the chart. How many people have got birthdays in the same month?

His birthday is **in** November.
It's **on** the 12th of November.

Her birthday is **in** July.
It's **on** the 5th of July.

2 Favourite months   vocabulary; discussion

Which months are good months for you? Which months aren't very good? Choose these words or find some others in the dictionary. Put the words on the chart.

quiet   busy   interesting   boring
cold   hot   beautiful weather   terrible weather

Compare with a partner.

Example: A: *Which months are your favourites?*   B: *May and December.*
A: *Why?*   B: *Well, the weather is beautiful in May.*

Now ask two or three other learners.

REVIEW OF UNIT 1

1 The car park is at the end of the street   saying where things are; writing sentences and guessing

Look at these expressions. Check that you understand them.

> next to   opposite   across from   on the left   on the right
> on the ground floor   on the first floor   on the second floor   one floor up
> one floor down   along the corridor   at the end of the corridor
> at the end of the street

Work with a partner. Write four sentences – some of them true, and some of them false – to say where things are in the school or in the city or town.

Example: 1. *In our school, the toilets are on the second floor, opposite the lifts.* (True)
2. *In our city, the cinema is next to the supermarket.* (False)
3. *The Principal's office is on the ground floor, at the end of the corridor.* (False)
4. *The car park is next to the school.* (True)

Read your sentences to the class. Ask them: are the sentences true or false?

2 Where's the Director's office, please?   listening; creative writing

⬛ Listen and tick (✓) the expressions you hear.

next to ......   on the right ......   opposite ......

across from ......   along the corridor ......   on the left ......

one floor up ......   one floor down ......   at the end of the corridor ......

What happens next? With a partner continue the story. Tell your ending to other learners.

Example: *Knock, knock. Come in!*

3

WHAT WOULD YOU LIKE TO EAT?

Language focus:
present simple question forms
the verb *to have* (used with meals, food and drink)
asking what people would like and saying what you'd like
countable and uncountable nouns

Vocabulary:
food and meals, prices

A

1 What do you have for breakfast? | vocabulary; discussion

tea

1 .... 2 .... A

3 .... B

C

D

4 ....

Is your breakfast like one of these? Do you have other things for breakfast? Add them.
Add the four missing words:

bananas   eggs   milk   coffee

Listen to the recording. Match each speaker with one table.

Speaker 1: Table ....   Speaker 2: Table ....   Speaker 3: Table ....   Speaker 4: Table ....

Three things are in the pictures but not on the recording. What are they?

..............................., ... and ....

Compare your ideas about breakfast. Ask and answer questions with a partner.

Example: A: *What do you have for breakfast?*
B: *I have coffee and toast. What about you? Do you have a big breakfast?*
A: *No, just tea and cereal. What time do you have breakfast?*
B: *About seven.*

HELP

What do you have for breakfast? Nothing.
What do you have for breakfast at the weekend?
Link questions: How about you? What about you?
What about your ... parents? friends? children?

Ask others in the class:

– What's a good breakfast for adults? What's a good breakfast for children?

2 Room Service

What would you like? / What time would you like breakfast?; I'd like ...

BREAKFAST
MENU
❖
Fruit juice
❖
Cereal
❖
Eggs:
fried, scrambled or boiled
sausage, tomato
❖
Toast
❖
Coffee or tea

▱▱ ▱▱ The double ▱▱ ▱▱ here and in other parts of the book means that there are two recordings of the listening: an easier one and a more difficult one. Decide which one to listen to, or listen to both.

Listen to someone on the telephone to Room Service. Write down his room number, his breakfast order and his breakfast time.

Check your notes with a partner. Then practise a room service order with your partner.

Example: A: *Room Service. What would you like?*
B: *I'd like to order breakfast, please.*
A: *What's your room number?*
B: *It's .... I'd like some ....,*
   and some ....
A: *What time would you like your breakfast?*
B: *At ...., please.*

ROOM	SERVICE	
Room number	Meal order	Time

3 I'd like some sugar, please countable and uncountable nouns

Some things are counted. The nouns for these things are called *countable nouns*.
Example: *I'd like one egg, two eggs, three eggs.*

Some things are not counted. The nouns for these things are called *uncountable nouns*.
Example: *I'd like some rice.* (**not** ~~one rice, two rices~~)

Put the nouns in the box into two groups, under these headings:

Countable nouns   *Uncountable nouns*

apple	sugar	rice	peach	water	milk	banana	cheese	tea
noodle	toast	cereal	butter	yoghurt	fruit juice	bread	orange	

Check your answers in groups. Then look at these two examples.

1. a banana (countable):
   There's a banana on the table. There are bananas in the shops.
   I'd like a banana, please. I'd like some bananas, please.
   How many bananas would you like? I'd like four bananas, please.

2. rice (uncountable)
   some rice (*not* ~~one rice, two rices~~)
   There's rice in the shops. (*not* ~~there are rice~~)
   I'd like some rice, please. *or* I'd like a kilo of rice, please.
   How much rice would you like? (*not* ~~How many rices~~)

Complete the rules. Add examples.

Countable nouns
With countable nouns, use: *a* or ...., numbers or ....
Example: ....
Countable nouns are singular or plural.
Example: *one* ...., *two* ...., *three* ....
For questions, use: *How* ....? with countable nouns.
Examples: ....

Uncountable nouns
With .... nouns, use: .... article or *some*.
Example: ....
Uncountable nouns are never ....
Example: ....
For questions, use: How ....?
Example: ....

Check your answers with others.

4 What would you like for breakfast, madam? speaking practice; writing

With a partner, correct the mistakes in this dialogue.

WAITER: What would you like for breakfast, madam?
MOTHER: I'd like a cereal, and some coffee. With hot milks, please.
            And my daughter would like two egg, some apple, some toast with
            butters and a glass of water.
DAUGHTER: No, no, mother. No eggs, please. I'd just like a banana and some roll – with jam.

📖 Listen and check your answers. Practise the dialogue together. Now write a
dialogue with at least two mistakes. Ask others to correct them and read the dialogue.

QC Now do the **Quick Check** exercises your teacher will give you.

B

1 Today, we've got onions, lettuce and cucumber

learning vocabulary

Study the words and pictures.

▭ Listen, then study the words and pictures for two minutes.

Shut your books. Write down the food names you remember.

Compare your lists with others. Which food groups are easy to remember? Why?

2 My favourite food's ice cream

vocabulary; conversation

Use a dictionary. Add one new item to each group in the picture in Exercise 1.

– What's your favourite food? Is it good for you?

▭ Listen to two people talking. What's their favourite food?

Speaker 1: .... Speaker 2: ....

Ask other people about their favourite food.

Example: A: *How about you? What's your favourite fruit?* B: *Strawberries.*

3 What would you like to drink?

vocabulary practice; discussion

Imagine that some English friends or business associates are in your town for a visit. Work in a group of two or three. Think of a special meal to have with them.

Is your meal … dinner in a restaurant? dinner at someone's house? a picnic?

Make two lists:

List 1 (food, special dishes)   List 2 (things to drink)

Talk about your meal with other groups.

Example: – *Our meal's .... What about your meal?*
         – *We've got nice things to drink, for example ....*

Now imagine the meal. In your groups, discuss how to:

– describe the food to the English guests.
– ask what they would like to eat or drink.

QC Now do the **Quick Check** exercises your teacher will give you.

> **HELP**
> It's got meat and rice.
> It's a salad.
> It's a cold dish.
> It's spicy.

C

1 How much is milk in your country? | talking about prices |

How much are these things in your country?

Example: A: *How much is milk?*
        B: *It's about* .... (dollars, yen, marks) *a bottle / a litre.*

> **HELP**
> I've no idea.
> I'm not sure.

milk   bananas   mineral water   tomatoes   butter   eggs

Add two items to the list. Compare your ideas with others.

2 Is food cheap in your country, or expensive? | listening; discussion |

Is food cheap in your country or expensive? Listen to two people answering this question. Fill in the missing information.

	Cheap food	*Expensive food*
Speaker 1	....	....
Speaker 2	....	....

Compare your answers with other learners. What about your city or country? What food is cheap? What food is expensive?

3 I'm sorry, we haven't got any | role play |

You are in a market. Divide the class into two: sellers and shoppers.

Sellers: Make a list of the things you sell. Shoppers: Make a list of things to buy. Then find a seller and ask for the things on your list.

Shoppers:	*Sellers:*
Have you got any chocolates/ rice/coffee/olives/salmon?	Yes, madam. Yes, sir. *or* I'm sorry, we haven't got any. But we've got some nice ....
How much is it? How much are they?	It's only ...... (£, pence) today. Top quality. They're ...... (£, pence) a kilo. Really nice.
I'd like … a large box of ......, please	
How much is it altogether?	Here you are. Anything else? That's (£2).

QC Now do the **Quick Check** exercises your teacher will give you.

> **PERSONAL STUDY WORKBOOK**
> - exercises to help you remember the vocabulary of food and meals
> - some pronunciation work
> - more practice with plurals, and with countable and uncountable nouns
> - practice with *this, that, these* and *those*
> - reading and listening exercises about Asian food
> - another page of your visual dictionary – food

REVIEW OF UNIT 1

1 He's a dentist, and she's an engineer | vocabulary – jobs; pronunciation – sentence stress |

Look at the jobs. Make sure you understand them. Use a dictionary or ask others.

> actor/actress   doctor   teacher   builder   waiter/waitress   lawyer   dentist
> salesperson   engineer

Make one sentence with each of the jobs. Check your answers with others.

Example: *I'm an actor. I'm a doctor.*

Look at the stress pattern of this sentence:

● ● ●●

I'm an actor.

Which sentences are like 1. ●●●● 2. ●●●●● 3. ●●●●●?

▭ Listen and check your answers. Repeat the sentences if you wish.

2 Are dentists very expensive? | discussion; listening |

For an average family, in your country, how expensive are:

> dentists?   lawyers?   doctors?   plumbers?   builders?   car mechanics?

Guess. Are they expensive in the United States? Sri Lanka? Northern Ireland? In the green boxes, put E (very expensive or expensive), QC (quite cheap) or C (cheap).

COUNTRY \ JOB	doctors		dentists		lawyers		car mechanics, builders, etc.	
United States								?
Sri Lanka								
Northern Ireland						?		

▭ Listen to three people talking. Add E, QC or C in the yellow boxes. Are your ideas the same as the speakers'? Compare with a partner.

REVIEW OF UNIT 2

1 Some change for a phone call | group dictation; structure review; sound discrimination |

▭ Listen and write down the words you hear. Compare your answers in groups. Then listen again. With your group, make sure that your dialogue is correct.

2 Where are the ...? | group dictation |

▭ Listen and write down the words you hear. Compare with others in your group. Then listen again. With your group, make sure that your dialogue is correct.

4

A SENSE OF COLOUR

Language focus:
more question forms with present simple verbs:
Where do you ...? Why do you ...? How often do you ...? + present simple verb
introduction to present simple verbs in positive sentences
– 1st and 3rd person forms

Vocabulary:
clothing, colour
time expressions:
never, once a year, twice a year

A

1 100% cotton made in Portugal

vocabulary and conversation; listening

How many of these clothes are there in your classroom today? With a partner, make a list under these headings.

Items   Number in class   Colour

📼 Listen to three people talking about their clothes. Fill in the missing information

	Clothes mentioned	Colour	Made in	Made of
Julia	....	....	....	....
Mark	....	....	....	....
Suheila	....	....	....	....

What about the clothes in your class?

– What are they made of?
– Where are they from? Which countries are on the labels you can see?

HELP

a suit
socks
a coat
trousers
a T-shirt

Work in groups. Ask and answer questions.

Example: A: *Where's your jacket from?*
            B: *It's from Brazil. What's on the label of your tie?*
            A: *100% silk. Made in China.*

Now tell the class about one item of clothing.

Example: A: *Mario's got jeans made in the U.S.A. They're made of cotton.*

HELP
cotton
wool
silk
leather
nylon

2 Are some of your clothes old?   vocabulary; conversation

International organisations ask for clothes to help people in an emergency. What old clothes have you got at home? Think about these kinds of clothes. Make a list.

     summer clothes   winter clothes   children's clothes

Compare your list with a partner.

Example: *I've got a lot of old shirts – some summer shirts, and some winter shirts. And I've got one old jacket and some trousers. I haven't got any children's clothes. What about you?*

3 Pink uniforms for the police   vocabulary of colours; discussion

White
Pink
Red
Orange
Yellow
Purple
Blue
Green
Brown
Grey
Black

Choose some clothes from the shop window. Choose colours for the clothes. Compare your choices with others.

Example: A: *I'd like a black T-shirt and some black trousers. How about you?*
            B: *Black? No, not for me. I'd like a green blouse and a yellow skirt.*

What are good colours for these clothes?

clothes for children   clothes for winter   clothes for summer   casual clothes for women
casual clothes for men   formal clothes for men   formal clothes for women

What colour are these clothes in your country? Choose a new colour for them.

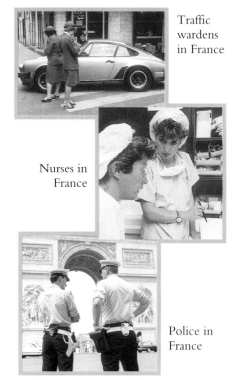

Traffic wardens in France

	Colour now	New colour
Uniforms for police	....	....
Uniforms for traffic wardens	....	....
Uniforms for nurses	....	....

Other uniforms in your country:

....	....	....
....	....	....

Nurses in France

Compare your choices. What colours are popular for uniforms in your class?

Have you got anything in an unusual colour? Tell the class about it.

For example: *yellow shoes   a pink car   an orange telephone   a blue cat*

QC Now do the **Quick Check** exercises your teacher will give you.

Police in France

B

1 Where do you buy your clothes? | listening; question forms |

Study the questions:

Where **do** you buy your clothes?   Where **do** they buy their clothes?
Where **does** he buy his clothes?   Where **does** she buy her clothes?

Now listen to three people. Make notes under the headings below.

	What does he/she buy?	Where does she/he buy clothes?
Speaker 1	....	....
Speaker 2	....	....
Speaker 3	....	....

Check your answers with a partner. What does each speaker buy and where?

2. How often do you buy shoes? | present simple questions and answers; time expressions; *because* |

Work in groups of three. Choose two or three questions to ask your partners. Make notes about their answers.

Questions	*Possible answers*
Where do you buy your shirts?	I buy my shirts at (from) the supermarket.
Where does your wife buy her jackets?	She buys her jackets from a shop called ....
Where does your husband buy his shoes?	He buys his shoes at the market.
Where does your friend buy her jeans?	She buys them at the department store.
Why?	Because they've got good quality clothes.
How often do you buy skirts?	About once a year / twice a year.
How often do you buy ties?	Three times a year.
How often does he buy socks?	Every year / every two years.

> **HELP**
>
> Never.
> My wife (my husband / my friend) buys them for me.

3 She buys her blouses in a department store | present simple: 3rd person |

Look at the examples. Then tell the class one thing about one of your partners.

Examples: *Julia buys her shoes at the market because they've got interesting shoes. She never buys hats. Her husband buys them for her.*

Alex never buys clothes. His wife buys them for him.

4 Where does Alex buy clothes? | practice with the 3rd person form; listening |

Look again at the examples in Exercises 1, 2 and 3. Now complete the following sentences by adding *do* or *does*, *buy* or *buys*.

1. Where .... you buy your ties, Lee?
   I .... them at the market, because they're cheap and colourful.
2. I .... my shoes from a department store, but my mother .... her shoes at the market.
3. How often .... Leah buy jackets?
   She .... jackets twice a year – in the summer, and in the winter. I sometimes .... a jacket in the winter – never in the summer.
4. Where .... your parents .... their clothes?
   They .... clothes from Marks and Spencer's, but they .... shoes from a little shoe shop near their house.
5. Do you and your friend .... your hats at the same shop, Franz?
   No, of course not! I .... my hats at the supermarket. She .... her hats at a hat shop, or sometimes at the market.

📖 Compare your answers with others. Then listen and check your answers.

QC Now do the **Quick Check** exercises your teacher will give you.

C

1 Red means money or good luck
3rd person singular; *means*; writing

Complete two or three of the sentences below about colours.

Example: *In English, to be blue means to be sad. In Ireland, green is the national colour and it means good luck.*

In ...., (*my country or my language*) red means ....

In ...., black means ....   In ...., white means ....

In ...., purple means ....   In ...., blue means ....

Compare your sentences in groups. Have you got the same or different meanings for colours?

2 What colour are roses?
speaking; reading

Answer these questions. Talk with a partner about your answers.

– What colour are roses?
– Are roses popular in your country?
– Are there any songs about roses in your country?

– How often do you buy roses? Who for?
– How often do you receive roses? Who from?

Read the text.

The rose is a very popular flower all over the world. Roses are in the books of Shakespeare and Dante, in the gardens of China and Japan. Roses are favourite gifts from men to their girlfriends or wives, and women also give roses to their family and friends. Roses mean many things: *I love you, thank you, I'm sorry.*

There are roses in many colours – red, white, pink, yellow, purple. And now there is a lot of interest in a new flower – the blue rose. Cut flowers are an important business – many billions of dollars worldwide – so new blue roses mean a lot of money in the future. In Melbourne, Australia, scientists say that blue roses are almost ready for the flower shops.

There are many songs about roses: *My love is like a red red rose* and *Red roses for a blue lady.* Or is it now: *My love is like a blue blue rose* and *Blue roses for a red lady*? Probably not, because a new rose is exciting, but it's not so easy to change the colour of songs!

Write down one interesting thing from the article.

Find part of a sentence in the text which means the same as these sentences:

1. Many people give roses to the people they love.
2. Many people around the world make money by selling cut flowers.
3. Songs with colours in them are hard to change.
4. People in many countries love roses.
5. People give roses for different reasons.

QC Now do the **Quick Check** exercises your teacher will give you.

PERSONAL STUDY WORKBOOK

- pronunciation work
- question forms using present simple verbs
- a listening exercise about colours in different countries
- a reading text about blue jeans
- visual dictionary – clothes

REVIEW OF UNIT 2

1 Lost and found   listening

[] Listen to three people describing a lost bag. Put the words in columns 1 and 2.

	What colour is it?	What's it made of?	What kind of bag is it?
Speaker 1	....	leather	....
	....	....	....
Speaker 2	bright red with a white shoulder strap	....	....
Speaker 3	....	fabric with a bit of leather	....

black
 red
 white
   blue
brown

leather
    plastic
 fabric

Now listen as the recording continues and fill in column 3. Check your answers with others.

2 At home, I've got a very big suitcase   writing sentences; speaking

Think of a bag you've got at home.
Describe it on a piece of paper.

> What colour is it? ....
> What's it made of? .... (Make a drawing.)
> What's in it? ....

Now form groups of four or five. Swap papers so that everyone has a different piece of
paper. Ask questions to find your bag.

Example: A: *Have you got my bag?*   B: *What colour is it?*   A: *It's black.*

REVIEW OF UNIT 3

1 What is good with rice?   vocabulary; listening

1. What kinds of food are good to eat with these things?
   With a partner, list as many as possible.   fish   rice   chicken

2. [] Read the menu. Listen to the conversation.

The International Chicken Restaurant

★ ★ ★ ★ ★ *NOTHING BUT CHICKEN!* ★ ★ ★ ★ ★

Starters	*Main courses*	*Desserts*
Chicken soup with noodles	Roast chicken with potatoes and carrots	Egg custard
Chicken with plum sauce	Chicken with honey sauce	
Chicken pâté with toast	Chicken pie with peas and chips	
Chicken satay	Chicken curry with lime chutney	
	Chicken fried rice	
	Chicken kebabs with black olives	

With a partner, write a menu with only one kind of food. Then change partners.
Role play a scene like the one on the recording.

GOOD HABITS, NEW ROUTINES?

Language focus:	Vocabulary:
present simple verbs: positive, negative, questions	daily routines
frequency adverbs	habits and customs

A

1 Are you a morning person? | present simple verbs – 1st, 2nd person |

Think about the first hour of your day. Tick what you usually do.

A		B	
get up quickly	have a good breakfast	wake up slowly	don't have breakfast
sing in the bathroom	get dressed quickly	lie in bed and think	read a newspaper
talk to people	start work quickly	don't talk to people	start work slowly

Find out: are you a morning person? Ask your teacher.

2 First thing in the morning | present simple practice |

Make some questions using expressions from the box in Exercise 1. Ask another
learner the questions. Add a question about the weekend.

Example: A: *Do you usually have a good breakfast in the morning?*
B: *Yes, I do. / No, I don't. Not usually.*
A: *What about on Sunday?*
B: *Oh, I have a big breakfast.*

> **HELP**
>
> It depends.
> I don't have time.

---

3 She has a cup of coffee   `present simple – 3rd person`

This is what two people do first thing in the morning. With a partner, guess the order, then write 1, 2, 3, etc. in front of each sentence.

Speaker 1

..... She has two cups of coffee.

..... She has a bath.

..... She goes straight to the bathroom.

..... She has a slice of toast.

Speaker 2

..... He has a quick wash.

..... He goes back to the bathroom.

..... He makes breakfast.

..... He gets dressed.

..... He has a shower.

..... He goes to the bathroom.

..... He goes downstairs.

..... He leaves the house.

..... He has tea and two slices of toast.

▭ Listen to the two people. Check your guesses.

QC Now do the **Quick Check** exercises your teacher will give you.

B

---

1 How often do you sleep with the lights on?   `vocabulary and conversation; frequency adverbs`

How often do you do these things? Never? Sometimes? Often? Show your answer: stand against the wall.

How often do you:

– eat in bed?	– sleep with the lights on?	– listen to loud music?	– tidy your room?
– eat between meals?	– smoke at work?	– do the washing up?	– sing in the bathroom?

Think about two other habits. Ask a partner about them.

Example: A: *How often do you read at mealtimes?*
B: *Never. I don't think it's a good habit.*

Make a list of your habits (things you do often). Write sentences.

Example: *I often smoke at work **and** listen to loud music.*
*I often eat in bed **but** I never sleep with the lights on.*

Compare your habits with other learners.

Examples of questions to ask:

– What habits have you got?   – Have you got any good habits?   – Have you got any bad habits?

2 It's a very bad habit!   writing a conversation; listening; speaking

Put the bubbles in the right order. Write sentences in the empty bubbles to complete
the conversations.

> Well, it's a very bad habit.

> Don't you? Oh, I eat little snacks all day.

> I don't eat between meals.

> Have a chocolate.

> You talk and talk. You never listen.

> But I don't talk a lot at all. I really don't.

> Well, you never listen.

Now listen to two conversations. Write down the last sentences. Compare them
with your sentences.

Listen to Conversation 1 again. With your partner, practise saying it. When you are
ready, have a short conversation about your own habits.

Example: A: *Do you watch television a lot?*   B: *Yes, sometimes.* (**or** *No, I don't. No, never.*)
A: *I think it's relaxing, don't you?*   B: *Yes, I do.* (**or** *No, I don't. Not really.*)

3 Language learning habits   discussion; listening; writing; asking questions

What do you do to learn English? Tick the sentences. Add other sentences.

To learn English, I …

...... use my dictionary.
...... write down new words.
...... translate new words into my language.
...... read English newspapers or books.
...... talk in English.
...... listen to English songs.
...... sing English songs.

....

....

Work in groups of three. Compare your ideas about language learning.

Example: A: *I use my dictionary a lot, and I always write down new words. What about you?*
B: *No, I don't write down words. But I talk in English a lot, and I listen to English songs.*

Listen to a teacher of English talking about her students, and their language
learning habits. The names of her students are Pedro, Ruiko, Susanna and Otto.

Are these statements true or false?

1. Pedro uses his dictionary a lot.
2. Pedro doesn't write down new words.
3. Ruiko writes down new words in one book, then
   she writes them again with different colours.
4. Ruiko doesn't write a translation for new words.
5. Susanna doesn't write anything.
6. Susanna doesn't talk in English.
7. Otto doesn't talk much in class.
8. Otto listens to English songs, but
   he doesn't sing them.

Write three questions about language learning habits. Ask other people in the class
your questions.

Example: *Do you read newspapers in English?*

QC Now do the **Quick Check** exercises your teacher will give you.

1 People kiss on both cheeks

practice with present simple verbs; conversation

With a partner, match the pictures with the sentences.

1. People take off their shoes to go into a house.
2. Men shake hands.
3. Men and women kiss on both cheeks.
4. People eat food with only their right hand.
5. People eat a special cake on their birthday.
6. People stand in queues.

Do you know any countries where people have these customs?

1. *Japan*
2. ....
3. ....
4. ....
5. ....
6. ....

Talk about your answers with other learners.

Example: A: *Do people eat food with their right hand in your country?*
B: *Yes, we do. We never eat food with the left hand. What about in your country?*

Do you know any other interesting customs from other countries? Work in small groups and tell each other.

2 How often do you go shopping?

more frequency adverbs; listening and speaking

Choose one of the expressions and complete the sentence:

I go shopping ....

every day   once a day   twice a week   every week
three times a month   every month   four times a year

every day

every week

every month

Compare your answers with others.

🔲🔲 Listen to people from different countries. How often do they go shopping? Complete the sentences.

Speaker 1 goes shopping *once a week* ....

Speaker 2 goes ....

Speaker 3 ....

Speaker 4 ....

Compare your sentences with two other learners. Then talk about your own shopping habits. Use these questions if you like.

How often do you go shopping?   Where do you buy vegetables? Clothes?
How often do you buy clothes?   What do you buy every day?

3 What do you do in a long queue? speaking

People queue in some countries. Do you queue in your country? Where? Tick the correct columns in the table.

	always	*often*	*sometimes*	*never*
banks	......	......	......	......
post offices	......	......	......	......
cinemas	......	......	......	......
food shops	......	......	......	......
supermarkets	......	......	......	......
....	......	......	......	......

Compare your answers with others.

Do you think queuing is a good thing or a bad thing? What do you do in a long queue? Do you read? Do you talk to people?

4 Q – a poem reading

▭ Fill in the empty thought bubble. Read the poem, then listen to it on the recording.

Q

I join the queue.
We move up nicely.

I ask the lady in front
What we are queuing for.
'To join another queue,'
She explains.

'How pointless,' I say,
'I'm leaving.' She points
To another queue.
'Then you must get in line.'

I join the queue.
We move up nicely.

Roger McGough

We're moving up nicely.

QC Now do the **Quick Check** exercises your teacher will give you.

PERSONAL STUDY WORKBOOK

- present simple verbs
- question forms
- a listening exercise about routines and habits
- reading texts about a police doctor and about videos
- visual dictionary – daily routines

REVIEW OF UNIT 3

1 **Visiting someone's home** | reading |

Talk about these questions with a partner.

1. Do you give a gift on your first visit to a person's home?
2. Do you give one gift only, or do you give an even number of gifts (2, 4, 6, 8, etc.)?
3. Does the host return some of the gifts to you?
4. Are some gifts a sign of happiness and good luck?
5. Are some gifts a sign of bad luck, sadness, or even death?
6. Is it OK to give a gift of any colour, or are some colours not OK?

Read this article about visiting someone's home.

Answer these questions:

– Which country is the article about?
– Find answers to the six questions above.

Check your answers with others.

Work with a partner. Think of these situations.

1. Someone invites you to dinner at their house. In your country, what are good gifts to take? Write down two ideas.
2. You go to stay at someone's home. In your country, what are good gifts to take? Write down two ideas.

Compare your ideas with others in the class.

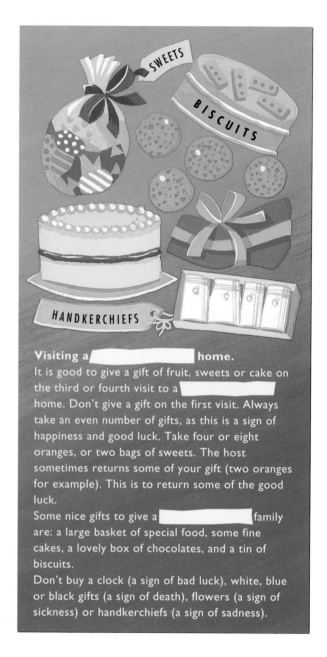

Visiting a _____ home.

It is good to give a gift of fruit, sweets or cake on the third or fourth visit to a _____ home. Don't give a gift on the first visit. Always take an even number of gifts, as this is a sign of happiness and good luck. Take four or eight oranges, or two bags of sweets. The host sometimes returns some of your gift (two oranges for example). This is to return some of the good luck.

Some nice gifts to give a _____ family are: a large basket of special food, some fine cakes, a lovely box of chocolates, and a tin of biscuits.

Don't buy a clock (a sign of bad luck), white, blue or black gifts (a sign of death), flowers (a sign of sickness) or handkerchiefs (a sign of sadness).

REVIEW OF UNIT 4

1 **I wear jeans at home after work** | vocabulary consolidation; discussion |

What do you wear at work? at home after work? on holidays? for parties or weddings? Talk about your choices with others in the class.

Example: *At home, I wear casual clothes – jeans, and a shirt. At work, I wear a suit. I wear bright colours at home, but dark colours at work.*

Are casual clothes popular in your country? Which ones? Do old people wear casual clothes, for example jeans or T-shirts, or do they wear formal clothes?

2 **We wear whites and we wear greens** | pronunciation: sentence rhythm, /v/ and /w/ |

⫿⫿ Listen to the rhythm chant, then say it. Your teacher can give you a copy of the words. Half the class says part A, half the class says part B.

6

THE WAY YOU LOOK

Language focus:
expressing opinions; agreeing and disagreeing with opinions
I'd like for wishes
adjectives and modifiers
too and *not enough*

Vocabulary:
appearance: face and body
describing personality

A

1 My friend looks serious but he's a lot of fun [vocabulary; speaking; listening]

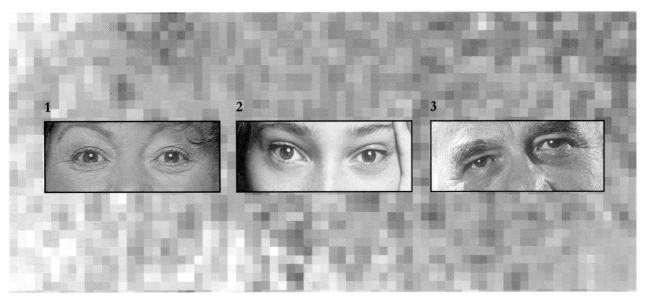

Look at the eyes in the pictures. What kind of people do you think they are?
Talk with a partner about your guesses.

Example: A: *I think Number 1's lively.*   B: *Me too.* (or *I think so, too.*)
          A: *Number 3 looks a bit sad.*   B: *Do you think so? I think he looks serious.*

You can use these words, or others. Use a dictionary to help you.

HELP
a bit
quite
very

sad   lively   kind   old   confident   practical   happy
serious   selfish   young   shy   artistic

Listen to their friends describing 1, 2 and 3. Write in the table the words
they use. Guess: which friend is 1? 2? 3?

	He's/She's	1, 2 or 3?
Speaker A's friend	*confident*	
Speaker B's friend	*practical*	
Speaker C's friend	*a lot of fun*	

Listen again. Confirm your guesses about 1, 2 or 3.

2 I'm a practical person, really   `speaking; adjectives`

Work in groups of three. Use adjectives from Exercise 1 to describe your partners'
personalities. Compare your ideas.

Example: A: *Bettina, I think you're very confident. You seem a lively person.*
B: *Really? I'm not very confident, really …*
A: *And Lazlo, I think you're very kind.*
C: *Yes, I think I'm quite kind. You're kind too, I think.*

3 Is your hair curly?   `vocabulary extension: adjectives; speaking`

What do parts of the face tell you about someone's personality? Try this questionnaire.
Tick the words that are appropriate for you. Use a dictionary to help you.

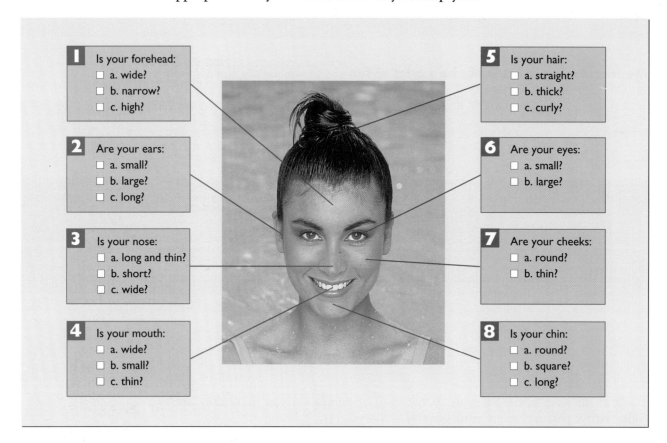

Now check your profile and tick the right letter.

Profile

1. a. – confident
   b. – ambitious
   c. – shy

2. a. – artistic
   b. – shy
   c. – serious

3. a. – serious
   b. – shy
   c. – kind

4. a. – artistic
   b. – kind
   c. – ambitious

5. a. – serious
   b. – lively
   c. – confident

6. a. – ambitious
   b. – lively

7. a. – lively
   b. – artistic

8. a. – confident
   b. – lively
   c. – kind

How many ticks in the profile have you got for each one of these words?

confident ☐   serious ☐   artistic ☐   ambitious ☐   lively ☐   shy ☐   kind ☐

Find your personality type.

Example: *Serious*
0 ticks – You are not serious at all.   *2 ticks – You are quite serious.*
1 tick – You are not very serious.   *3 ticks – You are very serious.*

Do the same for the other words you ticked. Compare your results with a partner. Do you agree with your personality profile? Discuss it with your partner.

Example: A: *Are you ambitious?*
B: *I've got two ticks. That means I'm quite ambitious.*
A: *Is that true?*
B: *Well, I've got a narrow forehead and small eyes, but I don't think I'm ambitious, really.*

QC Now do the **Quick Check** exercises your teacher will give you.

B

1 I'd like a child with brown eyes | vocabulary; speaking; listening |

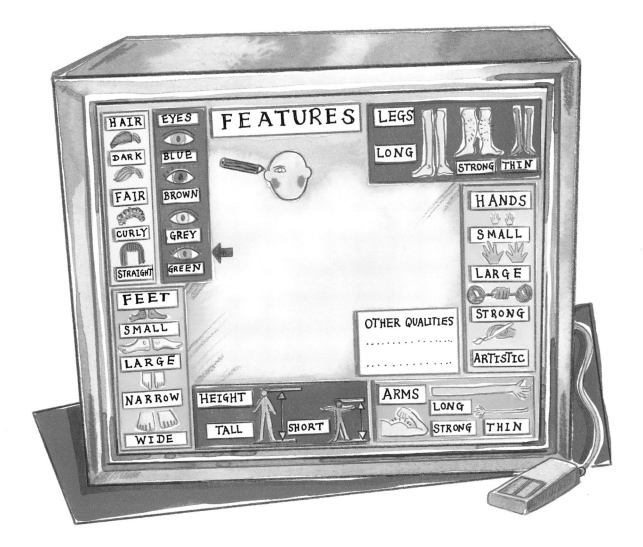

Imagine that it is possible to choose the way your child looks. Study the choices. Add others. Mark them on the computer. Then talk about your choices with a partner.

Example: *I'd like a child with dark, curly hair, blue eyes, long legs, small feet and strong arms. I think I'd like a tall child with artistic hands … and very intelligent, of course!*

HELP
intelligent
beautiful
a smiling face

📼 Listen to two people. Write down their choices.

Speaker 1 would like a girl with .... , ... and ....

Speaker 2 would like a boy with .... and ....

2 The sleeves are too long! | too and not enough; listening; dictation |

Study the picture and
the sentences.

The gloves are too small.
The gloves are not big enough.
My hands are too big.

Look at these three pictures.

A   B   C

📼 Listen to six sentences. Write them down. Match each sentence with a picture.

QC Now do the **Quick Check** exercises your teacher will give you.

C

1 Is it important for a friend to be lively? | vocabulary and speaking |

Complete these sentences. Choose expressions from the boxes or use other expressions.

For me, it's important for a friend to be ...., ... and ....

> lively   artistic   practical   kind   confident   a non-smoker

For me, it's important for a friend to be interested in .... and ....

> travel   an outdoor life   parties   music   cats   conversation   reading   TV

Talk about your choices with a partner.

2 Long-haired guy looking for interesting woman [reading]

These are personal advertisements from newspapers in Australia, England, America and Japan. Read the ads. Are any of them unusual? Tell your partner.

Young American man, 22, lively, artistic, seeks Japanese girl for friendship. Send photo or description to Box 88.

Very long-haired guy, 37, 5' 8", very thin, friendly, confident, smoker. Interested in parties, rock music. Has a home with two cats, looking for interesting woman. Box No. 96/83.

Family seeks young, confident girl to help with two lively children, Jeremy, 5, and Emma, 2½. Non-smoker, interested in travel and an outdoor life.

Man, 64, and woman, 43, plan October trip to Borneo, Brunei, Kuala Lumpur, Malaysia, Bangkok, Thailand and Hong Kong.
Are there friendly people in those places to meet for coffee/tea and good conversation? L. R. Duffy, 133 South Road, Newton, Pennsylvania 17809, U.S.A.

Are these sentences true or false? Write *T* or *F*.

..... There are two men under forty.

..... A family has two cats.

..... A man and a woman plan to go to Asia at the beginning of the year.

..... The children and the young American man are lively.

..... A Japanese girl seeks friendship.

..... The man with long hair is a non-smoker.

..... Two people ask for photos.

3 In reply to your ad, here is some information ... [writing a letter]

Answer one of the ads for a friend or for yourself.
Fill in the missing information.

Dear .... *,*
In reply to your ad in the .... *, here is some information about* .... *(me/my friend* .... *). I am (He/She is)* .... *years old, with* .... *hair and* .... *eyes. I am (He/She is)* .... *I am (He/She is) a smoker (a non-smoker). I'm (He/She is) interested in* .... *.*
Please write soon.
Yours sincerely,
....

Read your letter to others in the class.

QC Now do the **Quick Check** exercises your teacher will give you.

PERSONAL STUDY WORKBOOK

- vocabulary of appearance and personality
- pronunciation work
- a listening exercise about a job application
- a reading text about photographers and models
- writing descriptions of people
- visual dictionary – the body

REVIEW OF UNIT 4

1 How often do you go shopping?   `question forms with do`

Study these question forms with *do*.

	Do	you go away for your holidays?
When	do	you get up?
How often	do	you go shopping for food?
Where	do	you go?
What	do	you do in the evenings?

Add the missing words in these questions.

1. How often you buy clothes?
2. Do you shopping at the weekend?
3. When you play football?
4. What you wear in the winter?
5. Where do find good shoes?
6. Do you go the supermarket on Saturday?

Check your answers with a partner.

REVIEW OF UNIT 5

1 On Sundays, I ...   `vocabulary and collocation`

Here are ten jumbled sentences. With a partner, write ten correct sentences.

On Sunday mornings ...

1. I make the windows.
2. I kiss my room.
3. I feed the radio.
4. I eat the bed.
5. I smoke the children.
6. I listen to breakfast.
7. I wash the TV.
8. I tidy the cat.
9. I clean a cigarette.
10. I watch my clothes.

1. I make ....
2. I kiss ....
3. I feed ....
4. I eat ....
5. I smoke ....
6. I listen to ....
7. I wash ....
8. I tidy ....
9. I clean ....
10. I watch ....

2 I always listen to the radio   `speaking; listening`

What do you really do on Sundays? Ask your partner. Then tell another person what your partner does on Sundays.

Example: A: *What do you do on Sundays, Juan?*
B: *I always play football in the afternoon, and watch TV in the evening.*
A: *Juan always plays football in the afternoon on Sundays, and he watches TV in the evenings.*
C: *That's interesting. I never watch TV on Sundays.*

Listen to two people talking about what they do at the weekend. Fill in the table. Check your answers with others in the class.

Speaker 1 ....
Speaker 2 ....

7

WHAT CAN WE DO?

Language focus:	Vocabulary:
can for ability, skills or permission: positive, negative statements, questions	personal skills and abilities
can and *could* for requests	childhood
introduction of past simple of *to be*: positive, negative statements, questions	
introduction of past simple: *to have*, *to go*, positive statements only,	
and *could* as past tense of *can*	

A

1 Can you use a computer?   can, can't (ability/skills); vocabulary, reading and speaking

Read these questions with a partner. Use a dictionary to help you.

Can you ...	Yes	No
– read in a crowded train or bus?	......	......
– type with all your fingers?	......	......
– use a computer?	......	......
– repair a car?	......	......
– wash and iron your own clothes?	......	......
– cook a meal?	......	......
– ....?	......	......
– ....?	......	......

Add two more questions. Answer the questions for yourself. Compare your answers in groups.

Example: A: *Can you use a computer?*
B: *Of course I can, it's easy.*
B: *Can you repair a car?*
A: *No, I can't. It's too hard! Can you repair a car, Sara?*
C: *No, I can't. I take it to the garage.*

> **HELP**
> It's easy.
> It's too hard.

Which skills are important for you? Choose one or two. Ask about others' choices.

Example: A: *I can type. It's an important skill for me, because I'm a secretary. What about you – can you type?*
B: *No, I can't type. But I can repair a car, and that's important for me, because I use my car a lot.*

2 What can you do? | practice with *can* in questions; dictation |

guitar

drums

What can you do? Can you do anything special?

Example: *Can you play a musical instrument? (the drums, the guitar …) Can you write a poem? Can you remember poems? Can you draw or paint? Can you draw with a computer?*

Think of one thing you can do. If you can, think of an unusual thing. Write it down on a piece of paper. Ask the teacher for help if you have a problem.

Example: *I can play the drums.*

Now give your paper to the teacher. Write down the things people in your class can do, as the teacher dictates them. Now find out who can do these things in your class. Ask one person one question, then ask another person.

Example: A: *Renate, can you play the drums?*   B: *No, I can't.*
A: *Gerd, can you play the drums?*   C: *Yes, I can. I play in a band.*

What are some unusual activities in your class?

3 But can he use a computer? | grammar practice; reading and writing short dialogues or letters |

Read these three sentences.

1. I'm sorry, I can't repair this photocopier.
2. Dear Miss Sarenta,
   We are sorry that we cannot repair your photocopier.
3. I can play the guitar and my friend can play the drums – we play at parties for our friends.

Fill in the blanks with one appropriate word.

1.
'Can you read on your way to work, Mat?'
'No, I .... read in crowded buses at all, but my sister .... She .... a whole magazine on her way to work in the morning.'

2.
'Well, Mr Grestun seems right for the job. But .... he use a computer?'
'Oh, yes, he .... computers all the time now.'
'And .... he type?'
'Well, he .... type very well, I'm afraid. He types with two fingers – but he's very fast!'

3.
Dear Mrs Bosak,
I am very sorry indeed that we .... use your story in our magazine this week.

4.
Dear Deni,
I'm here in Nema with Sam and Lisa. Sam's a wonderful cook. He .... make lovely meals, but he takes a lot of time. So Lisa makes sandwiches for us at lunchtime.

Check your answers with a partner.

Now write a short dialogue or letter with blanks. Ask another pair to fill in the blanks.

QC Now do the **Quick Check** exercises your teacher will give you.

B

1 **At what age can you get married?** | *can* for permission |

You can drive a car in Australia at 16.   You can open a bank account in Canada at 7.   You can vote at 18 in England.

What about your country? At what age can you vote? drive a car? open a bank account? buy cigarettes? get married?

Check your answers with others – or compare answers if you are from different countries.

Listen to two people answering the questions for their countries. Write down their answers.

	Speaker 1	Speaker 2
At what age can they vote?	....	....
At what age can they drive a car?	....	....
At what age can they open a bank account?	....	....
At what age can they get married?	....	....

Check your answers with others. Are the speakers' countries like yours?

2 Can I try it on, please?

can and *could* for requests; *anybody* and *anywhere*

Who usually asks these questions? Where? Study the examples to see the meaning of *anybody* (any person) and *anywhere* (any place).

Question	Who?	Where?
1. Can I have 3 kilos of oranges, please?	A shopper	In a shop
2. Can I see your passport?	An official	At the airport
3. Could you tell me the time, please?	Anybody	Anywhere
4. Could you pass me the salt?		
5. Could you show me your book?		
6. Could you fill in the form, please?		
7. Can you wait for me?		
8. Can you get me a coffee, please?		
9. Could you write it on the board?		
10. Can you shut your books and listen to the cassette?		

QC Now do the **Quick Check** exercises your teacher will give you.

C

1 I was a happy child

the past simple tense; *could* as past tense; listening and speaking

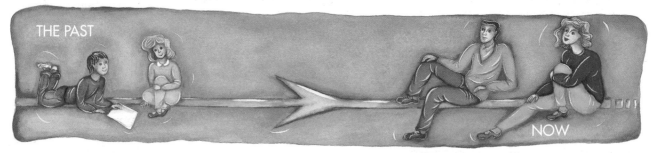

I was a very happy child.	I am quite a happy adult.
I wasn't very busy.	I am now very busy.
I went to school.	I go to work.
I had a lot of friends.	I have a lot of friends.
I could play all day.	I work all week – but I can relax on Sundays.

Study the sentences above. Are they true for you as a child? As an adult?

Listen to two people comparing themselves as children and as adults. Complete the notes.

	as a child	as an adult
Speaker 1		
Speaker 2		

Tell a partner about yourself as a child, and as an adult.

Example: A: *I was a happy and lively child. I had a lot of time. I could run and jump all day. Now I sit and work all day. I haven't got enough free time. I'm too busy. Is that the same for you?*
B: *No, I wasn't very happy. I was a lonely child, but now I've got a lot of friends.*

2 My father's life   reading; discussion

A Chinese family went to live in Canada. The teenage daughter is a student of English. She writes about her father. There are seven expressions in the box. Guess: are they about her father's life in China, or in Canada?

language problems   pay not very good   an easy life   a bank manager
school in the evening   a friendly boss   restaurant at lunchtime

Read the essay and check your guesses. (There are some mistakes in the student's English.)

In his new situation in Canada, and with the language problems, my father is not really in the right place. He cannot finds a good job, appropriate for him. He works with machines all the time. The pay is not very good, but he is happy because the boss is friendly. He can take an hour for lunch. In China, he went to a restaurant with his friends. Here, he reads a lot in his lunchtime. But he cannot reading English yet.

In China, my father was a bank manager. He had an easy life. Here, he works in a company, and he works very hard. He goes to school in the evening, so that he can studies English. After a whole day's work, how he can find enough energy to listen to the teacher? I don't know.

I ask my father: what do you expect from us in the future? He answers with a smile. He says it is enough if we can find good husbands and have good families. I don't think so. I know he wants us to be famous, to be doctors, or something useful like that.

In the text, there are four mistakes with the use of *can* or *cannot*.
Find them and correct them. You can work with a partner if you like.

Complete the answers to these questions.

1. Why is the father not in the right place? Because he cannot ....
2. Why does the father like his job? Because ....
3. Why does he go to school? To ....

Compare your answers with others.

Do you know anyone in a similar situation? What are the difficulties of people who come to live in your country?

3 In China he went to a restaurant with his friends <u>writing</u>

Write three sentences. Compare the father's life in China and in Canada.

Example: *In China, he went to a restaurant for lunch, but in Canada, he reads at lunchtime.*

QC Now do the **Quick Check** exercises your teacher will give you.

PERSONAL STUDY WORKBOOK

- *can* – statements and questions
- pronunciation work – weak forms
- an exercise comparing town and country
- practice in writing a summary
- visual dictionary – abilities

D REVIEW AND DEVELOPMENT

REVIEW OF UNIT 5

1 Annoying habits <u>vocabulary and speaking; listening</u>

Other people's habits can be very annoying. When do you get annoyed? Choose three of these or add your own:

I get annoyed when people:
- make a lot of noise when they eat.
- start work very slowly.
- don't wash up after meals.
- smoke in my house.
- don't listen when I speak.
- play loud music.
- watch TV all the time.
- drop litter.

Talk about your choices in groups.

CD Listen to two people talking about what annoys them. Make notes about each speaker. Check your answers with others.

2 I get to work at three <u>collocation</u>

Which of the expressions in the box can go with each verb?

Verbs
I get .... I have ....
I make ....

a cup of tea   a chat   a bath   home   an appointment   annoyed   a rest
to work   a phone call   up

Check your answers in groups. In turn, say a sentence about yourself, using one of the verbs.

Example: A: *I have a cup of tea first thing in the morning.*
B: *I get annoyed when people smoke in my house.*
C: *I usually make a phone call to my mother every evening.*

3 That's the way the day goes

pronunciation – rhythm and stress practice; weak form /ə/

Read a poem about a hard worker. Can you guess the missing parts?

I get up in the morning,
I have a cup of .... ,
I sit and read the paper,
I get to work at three.
So that's the way the day goes,
Yes, that's the way the day just ... goes.

I get a cup of coffee,
I tidy up my desk;
I look at all my letters,
It's time to have a ....
And that's the way the day goes,
Yes, that's the way the day just ... goes.

I make a few quick phone calls,
I write a word or two;
I have a chat with old friends,
I sit and think of ....
So that's the way the day goes,
Yes, that's the way the day just ... goes.

I get home in the evenings,
I'm tired, it's getting late;
I sit and watch a programme,
And go to bed at ....
And that's the way the day goes,
Yes, that's the way the day just ... goes.

▭ Listen and confirm your guesses. Complete the sentences. Listen to the poem again. This time you say lines 2 and 4 in each part.

REVIEW OF UNIT 6

1 A beard really changes your face!

vocabulary extension – appearance; speaking

With a partner, think of ways of changing your appearance. How many ways can you add? Use a dictionary or ask others.

Hair: Different hair style; new hair colour; ....
Face: Sunglasses; a beard or a moustache; ....
Cosmetics: ....
Clothes: A hat; high heels; ....
Jewellery: Earrings; ....

Compare your lists in groups.
What do you think about changing your appearance? Is it a good idea or a bad idea?

2 I think hats are really nice

writing

Write sentences to show your opinion.

Example: *I think big earrings are silly. Ears are nice as they are.*
              I thinks beards are really nice. They're a good way to change your face.
              I don't think a new hair colour is a good thing. Hair colour is bad for your hair, isn't it?

Work in groups. Read each other your sentences. Compare with other groups.

8

LOVE IT OR HATE IT!

Language focus:	Vocabulary:
talking about what you like or don't like	good and bad features of cities, countries and jobs
structure: verb + noun or verb + -ing form	pets

A

1 I like the energy | likes and dislikes: statements and questions; vocabulary; speaking |

Think about your town or city. Which of these things do you like about it? Add more things to the list.

> the markets   the cinemas   the street life   the river and bridges   the shops
> my house or flat   the parks   the restaurants   the people   the lifestyle
> the ....   the ....   the ....

Compare your views with a partner.

Example: A: *What do you like about this town?*
          B: *I like the markets and the small streets. What about you?*
          A: *The markets are not bad. The shops are good too, and I
             really love the cinemas.*

> **HELP**
> It's not bad.
> They're not bad.
> It's OK.
> They're OK.
> I quite like it/them.
> I like it/them.
> I love it/them.

Now think of things you don't like about your town or city. Use a dictionary and add to the list.

> the pollution   the crowds   the tourists   the traffic   the noise   the prices
> the heat   the cold
> the ....   the ....   the ....

Change partners and talk about your views.

Example: A: *What don't you like about your city?*
          B: *There's too much traffic. I don't like the noise and the pollution is terrible.*

> **HELP**
> I don't like it/them.
> I hate it/them.
> I really hate it/them.
> It's/They're terrible.

2 A sense of history? speaking and listening

What are the names of these four countries? What do you know about them?
Compare your ideas.

What do you think people like about these countries? Write your guesses on the red
lines.

	Country	I think people like …	The speakers like …
1.	....	....	....
2.	....	....	....
3.	....	....	....
4.	....	....	....

Listen to four people talking about the countries. Write notes on the blue lines.
Check your notes in groups. Compare your guesses and the speakers' ideas. Are there
any surprises?

3 What do you especially admire about the English? reading and discussion

What do you know about England and the English? Look at these questions – talk
about what you know – or what you can guess.

What do you like about the English?
What don't you like?
What do you especially admire?
What do you think of their sense of humour?

Read the article.
Complete this list of Lisa's opinions about the English.

What she likes
They are patient in queues.
....
....

What she doesn't like
the way they talk to poor people
....
....

Lisa Bergman is a Swedish journalist living in England.

What do you like about the English?
They are polite and friendly, especially out of London.

What don't you like?
The way they talk to poor people.

What do you especially admire about the English?
They are patient when they queue.

Are there things you really hate about them?
They say one thing but they do another!

What do you think of their sense of humour?
I love it very much.

Do you know England? If so, do you agree with Lisa?

Give scores to your own country (or the country you are in now). Use the same scores:
1 (really terrible) to 10 (very, very good).

Style: ....

Quick service from repair people: ....

Public transport: ....

Politeness of car drivers: ....

Politeness of people in shops: ....

.... : ....

.... : ....

Can you add other things to the list?

If you all come from the same country, do you all agree with each other? If you come from different countries, compare your scores with people from other countries.

Give these things a score on a scale of 1 (really terrible) to 10 (very, very good).

Style: 3
Quick service from repair people: 2
Public transport: 2
Politeness of car drivers: 5
Politeness of people in shops: 8

QC Now do the **Quick Check** exercises your teacher will give you.

B

1 I like the open spaces | *I like* + noun; *I like* + *-ing* form; writing questions; listening

Look at the answers to four questions. By yourself or with a partner, complete the four questions.

Question 1: What do you like about ....?
Answer: The buildings, the open spaces, the parks, the woodlands, the nightclubs, the fact that there are people from all over the world.

Question 2: What do you like about ....?
Answer: Getting presents, getting cards, having a party.

Question 3: What do you like about ....?
Answer: The view from the window, my bed, going to bed at night.

Question 4: What do you like about ....?
Answer: The women I work with, the pay, the holidays.

CD CD Listen to Lyn answering the four questions. Tick the things she likes in the answers above.

2 I really like having a party ⬚ speaking

Study the examples.

I like the parks.
the people.   *I don't like the traffic.*
the crowds.

I like walking in the parks.
speaking to the people.   *I don't like driving in the traffic.*
walking in the crowds.

▭ Now listen to the four questions in Exercise 1 again. Repeat them for practice.

Ask a partner the four questions. Make notes about the answers you hear.
Now change partners. Tell your new partner about your first conversation.

Example: *I like the restaurants in this city, but Inez likes the parks. I like getting presents for my birthday. Inez likes having a party and a special meal.*

3 They hate pushing trolleys ⬚ practice with verb + *-ing* form; writing and guessing

Match the pictures and the descriptions.

A

B

C

1. They like helping people but they don't really like working at night.
2. They like talking to people and answering questions, but they don't like adding up prices.
3. They like travelling and serving drinks, but they hate pushing the trolleys.

Write sentences about what people like doing in a job. You can choose one of these jobs or another one:

politicians   parents   English teachers   tourist guides

Read your sentences to others in a group or to the class. Don't say the name of the job. Can the others guess?

What about your own job? Are there things you don't like about it? Compare your views with others.

QC Now do the **Quick Check** exercises your teacher will give you.

C

1 I really hate spiders! | vocabulary and speaking |

Match the words and the
pictures.

Add at least two words to
complete these sentences.

I love .... and ....
I quite like .... and ....
I don't like .... and ....
I really hate .... and ....

Compare your sentences.
Then choose an animal as a pet
for these people.

Your English teacher
Two other people in your class
One of your friends
A member of your family

Compare your choices and
explain them.

goat   spider   goldfish   snake   cat   cockroach   canary
fly   tortoise   dog   horse   rat   mouse   mosquito

2 I like listening to pop music | speaking: fluency practice |

Look at this topic circle. Choose one topic and talk to a partner.

Here are some questions to ask and answer.

– What sort of .... do you like?
– What do you like about it (about them)?
– What don't you like about ....?
– Why do you like ....?
– Why don't you like ....?
– Do you like ....ing? What is hard about it? What is easy?

Build up some vocabulary lists for the topics. Use
some vocabulary from your conversations.

Examples:
Sports: tennis, hockey, baseball, basketball, ...

Flowers: rose, tulip, ...

Books: novels, cookery books, ...

Music: pop music, classical music, jazz, ...

Tell the class about your conversation.

sports

books

holidays

music

flowers

pets

colours

QC Now do the **Quick Check** exercises your teacher will give you.

PERSONAL STUDY WORKBOOK

- vocabulary of towns and animals
- pronunciation, speaking and listening exercises about likes
- a reading text about living in a different country
- writing a description for a tourist brochure
- visual dictionary – good and bad features of towns

REVIEW OF UNIT 6

1 My kitchen's too small | *too and not enough; writing a short description* |

Choose two things from your own life. Write a short description of them, saying what you don't like about them.

Example: *My kitchen is too small. There isn't enough space for a big fridge.*

In groups of three, read your sentences in turn. Ask the others questions.

Examples: A: *My kitchen is too small. What about your kitchen?*
B: *My kitchen's OK. It's big enough. But it's not very tidy.*
C: *My kitchen's much too small. There isn't enough space for two people!*

2 My bathroom's too dark | listening |

Listen to two people. Write 1 next to the things that Speaker 1 talks about, and 2 next to the things Speaker 2 talks about.

the bathroom's too small	....	not much light	....
not enough bedrooms	....	the garden	....
too many stairs	....	the living room	....

REVIEW OF UNIT 7

1 Can you come and feed the cat? | reading and writing requests |

Look at this example. Write what the person says in the other pictures, using *can.*

Example:

Read your sentences to another person. Together, prepare a role play of one of these situations. Perform your scene to your group or your class.

9

THOSE WERE THE DAYS

Language focus: past simple tense: consolidation of *be, have, do* regular verbs object pronouns	Vocabulary: memories of schooldays and the past

A

1 What can you remember?

practising simple past forms: *was/were, had*; reading

Answer these questions.

1. Can you remember at least five different telephone numbers?
2. What did you have for lunch three days ago?
3. What items of clothing did you have when you were about ten years old?
4. Can you remember all the words of your country's national song?
5. What was your favourite toy when you were a baby?
6. Can you remember anyone with glasses when you were a small child?
7. Who was your favourite actor or actress when you were 15?
8. Can you remember a special smell from your childhood?

HELP

I can't remember.

With a partner compare answers.

Example: A: *For lunch three days ago, I had some egg rolls. What did you have?*
B: *Mmm … I think I had a cheese sandwich.*

What kinds of things do you remember well? Do you remember things you see, things you eat, people or numbers? Are people in your class similar?

2 The smell of fresh grass

listening

🔲🔲 Listen to two people answering the questionnaire. Add the missing information in the diagram.

Check your answers in groups.

old secondary school. Was it

tions on the recording.

ese questions.

....

....

teacher? It was ....

ir and glasses — and a terrible temper.

....

....

ents around you? How many names
down.

s in small groups.

writing

riends — or someone in your family. Compare them as
are now.

), ... was .... She (He) was

.... She (He) ....

raphs to each other.

rcises your teacher will give you.

king and listening

the home addresses from the beginning of Helena's

What can you guess about Helena's life? Talk about it in groups.

Where was she born?

Where did she go to school?   In ...., then in ....

Where did she live after that?   She lived in ...., then in ....

What was her first job?   Maybe she was ....

What did she do then?   I think she ....

2 After that, I moved to Japan listening

▭ Look at the questions below. Can you answer any? Now listen to Helena talking about her life and her jobs. Check your guesses and complete the answers.

1. Where was she born?
   a. In England. b. In Italy. c. In India.
2. Where did she live until she was 18 years old?
   a. In a city. b. In a small village. c. In a town.
3. Where did she go after school?
   a. To a swimming pool. b. To a school in Malaysia.
   c. To an American camp for children.
4. What did she do when she finished school?
   a. She got a job. b. She went to university. c. She went to the States.
5. Where was she an English teacher?
   a. In the south of Japan. b. In England. c. In Nairobi.
6. After that what did she do?
   a. She trained as a teacher. b. She went to Cairo for three years.
   c. She didn't do anything.
7. What jobs did she do in England after that?
   a. She worked as a teacher. b. She worked in a bank and in publishing.
   c. She worked with children.
8. What was her job like?
   a. It was boring. b. She travelled a lot. c. She stayed at home.
9. Where did she go last month?
   a. Morocco. b. Uganda. c. Mexico.

3 Your time line speaking; writing

Here is a time line. Write some of the different home addresses from your life, the life of a friend, or a member of your family.

I was born   Now

Compare and talk about your time lines. Use the questions and the expressions in the box to help you.

Questions:
Where were you born?   Where did you go to school?
Where did you live when you were a child? Did you go to college or university?
Did you move a lot when you were a child? What was your first job?
When you moved, did you miss your old house?

was born   lived   moved   missed (my old house)   changed jobs   decided to stayed there for

Example: *Where did you live when you were a child?*
          When I was nine, we lived in Seville. Then we moved to Madrid.

Write a summary of your life, using the events on your time line.

Example: *I was born in* .... *. I lived in* .... *. Then I went to school in* .... *. After that,*
          I .... *.*

What strong memories do you have of your childhood home(s)? Share your memories with others.

Example: *I remember the garden … I remember my bedroom in our first house. It was at the back of*
          the house. There was an apple tree just outside my window …

▣ Now do the **Quick Check** exercises your teacher will give you.

1 I telephoned Mia yesterday from Hong Kong   reading and discussion

Put the expressions in the appropriate places.

an ankle   a hairstyle   a screen   bad handwriting   a broken ankle in plaster

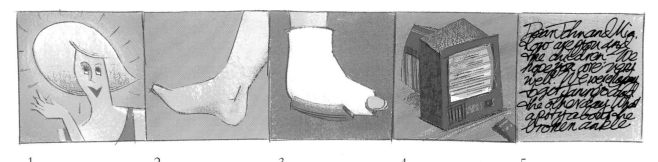

1 .... 2 .... 3 .... 4 .... 5 ....

Check your answers with others.

Read this extract from a diary. Does it seem strange to you? If so, why?

Choose the right answer.

1. Mia is the writer's
   a. mother.   b. wife.
2. Janine is the writer's
   a. daughter.   b. sister.
3. The writer has
   a. one child.   b. more than one child.
4. The writer lives
   a. in Hong Kong.   b. far away from Hong Kong.
5. The writer's parents live
   a. with him.   b. far away from him.
6. The writer works for
   a. a company.   b. the government.
7. The call was
   a. very expensive.   b. not very expensive.
8. I looked closely at her. Who did he look at?
   a. His mother.   b. Mia.
9. I tried to read some of it. What is it?
   a. His diary.   b. A letter from his parents.

14 Thursday

I telephoned Mia yesterday from Hong Kong. She was fine. Her new hairstyle looked great and the kids seemed fine too, apart from Janine's broken ankle. The plaster looked heavy on the screen but I'm sure it wasn't. Mia said I looked tired, but that's not surprising – I arrived in Hong Kong ten hours late. She showed me a letter from my parents and I tried to read some of it, but it was impossible to see all the words. My mother's handwriting is so bad these days. I'm sure the cost of that call was enormous. It's a good thing I can put it on the company account. When I looked closely at her, just before we finished talking, I noticed that she looked nervous about something. I wonder what it was.

Check your answers in groups.

What kind of phone did the writer use?
What do you think of this kind of phone?
Choose one of these pairs of people.

Boyfriend/girlfriend   Parent / teenage daughter or son   Boss/employee   You/...........

List the advantages (+) and disadvantages (–) of this type of phone for your pair.
Compare your views in groups.

2 I noticed that she looked nervous about something   pronunciation of past tenses; listening

🎧 Listen to the pronunciation of some past tenses. Write the verbs under these headings:

the verb ending = /t/	*the verb ending = /d/*
looked	telephoned

Now listen to the man reading his diary. The verbs are missing. Say the missing verbs.
Then listen to the full version and compare with your pronunciation.

3 It was a great day! | negatives with *didn't*; writing a diary with past tenses |

Think about yesterday. Make notes about these things.

Did you telephone anyone? (I telephoned … *or* I didn't telephone …)
Did you receive any phone calls? (I received … *or* I didn't receive …)
Who did you talk to? (I talked to … *or* I didn't talk to …)
Did you receive any letters? What happened yesterday? Did anything different or interesting happen?

Think of one or two words to describe yesterday. Use the words in the box if you like.

ordinary   extraordinary   boring   fantastic   great   pleasant   happy
frustrating   sad

Write a diary for yesterday. Talk about it with a partner.

Example: A: *Nothing happened. It was quite a boring day. What about you?*
          B: *I received a letter from my sister in Peru yesterday, so it was a nice day!*

QC Now do the **Quick Check** exercises your teacher will give you.

PERSONAL STUDY WORKBOOK

- past tenses of regular verbs
- little arguments – expressing disagreement
- listening to a sad story
- pronunciation work
- reading text – about a lucky catch
- visual dictionary – childhood memories

D   REVIEW AND DEVELOPMENT

REVIEW OF UNIT 7

1 Living in a new country | reading |

What do you think are the problems of people living in a new country? Talk about them with others.

Here are three different conversations about the problems of living in a new country. Which speakers are parents, and which are the young people?
Mark the statements **P** or **Y**.

1. A: ………… Why can't we speak English at home? I can't see any reason for that.

   B: ………… You can speak English outside if you want, but not here. You know I can't understand English.

2. C: ………… I have decided to go back home next month. Don't try to make me stay because you can't understand. I can't learn English.

   D: ………… Why can't you learn English? Susie and I can.

   C: Don't forget I am already sixty-eight – too old to start again. Dad and I are not in the right place here. We can't go shopping or visiting as you can, because we can't read the street names, we can't ask directions, we can't even answer the phone.

3. E: .... How lonely I am! Your mother and sister go to work. You go to school. I am alone at home with nothing to do. I can't go out because I have to look after the grandchildren.

F: .... Well, what about me? I'm lonely too. I talk with the other kids at school but I can't understand what they say. I still can't tell the difference between *can't* and *can*. To me they sound the same.

Check your ideas in groups, then with your teacher. Make a list of problems from the conversations.

Older people can't ...	Younger people can't ...
understand English	*understand other children at school*

What can the older people do to improve their English in the new country? Suggest two things. See how many ideas your class can find.

REVIEW OF UNIT 8

1 I like salmon pâté sandwiches | pronunciation practice: final 's' sound |

Listen to the lines.

1. He likes Ted. She likes Fred.
   He likes Ann. She likes Dan.
   I like ... holidays in the Mediterranean.
2. He likes rocks. She likes clocks.
   He likes bikes. She likes hikes.
   I like ... Jose.
3. He likes suits. She likes boots.
   He likes hats. She likes cats.
   I like ... salmon pâté sandwiches.

Read the final part and complete the last line – add something that you really like.

4. He likes rice. She likes ice.
   He likes meat. She likes wheat.
   I like ....

Now listen again and repeat. At the end, add your last line.

2 She likes trains | writing and practising rhymes |

By yourself or with a partner, create your own rhymes. Use these words, or your own:

He likes tea. She likes ....

He likes .... She likes trains.

I like ....

Go round the class, saying your lines in turn.

10

ONCE UPON A TIME

Language focus:
past simple: irregular verbs

Vocabulary:
stories and storytelling
books, films, TV programmes

A

1 Suddenly, a shot rang out | past simple irregular verbs; writing |

With a partner, look at the picture. Talk about it. Are any of these sentences the same as your reaction?

– I like railway platforms, even at night, because I like travelling.
– I think the railway platform is lonely. It's quite frightening.
– Well, it's night time. There's no one there. The picture's a bit sad, I think.

Write your own reaction here:

....

What do you think the first sentences of the story are? Choose a beginning from the next page, or write your own.

It was a dark and stormy night. Suddenly, a shot rang out.

....

....

The child sat and waited a long time. She ate all her sandwiches and thought sadly of home.

....

....

Continue your story. Choose a sentence or write your own.

1. 'What was that?' said James.
2. An old woman came towards her and said, 'Follow me.'
3. The train stopped suddenly and all the lights went out.

4. *Your sentence:* ....

....

Continue your story. Write at least one more sentence. Use the verb table on page 174 to help you. Then change partners. Tell each other your stories.

They met for the first time at a railway station. They did not speak to each other but caught the next train to …

....

....

2 She lit a match [listening]

Two people also chose sentences about the railway platform. Read their choices.

SPEAKER A: The child sat and waited a long time. She ate all her sandwiches and thought sadly of home. An old woman came towards her and said, 'Follow me.'

SPEAKER B: They met for the first time at a railway station. They did not speak to each other but caught the next train to Cairo.

The two people then continued the stories. Which of these sentences do you think each person used?

1. They walked down the street and turned into the doorway of a little cottage.
2. She lit a match.
3. The train stopped suddenly and all the lights went out.
4. He lit his cigarette with the match.
5. He panicked.
6. There was a fire burning and there was a lovely smell of something cooking in the oven.

☐☐ Listen to them telling their stories. Retell the stories with a partner.

Example: A: *What was the first story?*
B: *The child sat in the waiting room for a long time …*

3 I was born in South America `practice with irregular verbs`

Complete the table with the nouns in the box.

Noun	Present tense	Past tense
a birth	a baby is born	a baby was born
....	a person dies	a person died
....	a person meets another person	a person met another person
....	a person leaves another person	a person left another person
....	a person finds something	a person found something
....	a person loses or forgets something	a person lost or forgot something

> a loss   a discovery   a birth   a separation   a death   a meeting

Think of a real story about yourself, someone in your family, or a friend – a story with at least one of the things from the box in it.

Tell a partner your story. Then change partners. Tell each other two stories: your own story, and your first partner's story.

QC Now do the **Quick Check** exercises your teacher will give you.

B

1 I was born in Elorin   `listening`

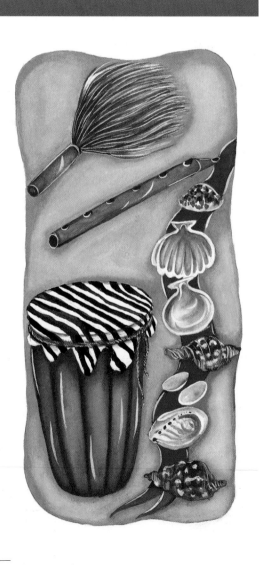

These are things used by a man for his job. What does he do for a living? Compare your ideas.

Listen to someone talking about Adesose Wallace and his job. Work with a partner.

Partner A: Take notes to answer these questions:

Where was Adesose born – what country? ....

What is his job? ....

What things does he do in his job? 1. He ....,
2. he plays musical instruments, 3. he ....
and 4. he does a bit of dancing.

Partner B: Take notes to answer these questions:

From which people did he learn his job? ....

When did they tell stories in his country? ....

Where did they tell stories in his country? ....

Where does he tell stories today? ....

Compare your notes and talk about them.

– Have you got storytellers in your country now? Were there any in the past?
– Are the storytellers in your country usually men or women? Are they usually old or young?

2 Ojumbala the rain god, and the seven children listening; reading

Match each picture with a sentence and put the sentences in the right order.

1. She ran to tell the old man the problem.
2. Long ago there lived an old man and his wife.
3. The mother found that there was no food in the house for the children.
4. They had seven children.

📖 Listen to the beginning of the story, and check your answers.

The story continues. Read Part 2.

The mother found food for the children. The father then called all the children together. He told them to stay inside the house. He told them not to go outside. The old man and the old woman left the children and went to the city.

📖 Listen to Part 2. What do you think happened next? Did the children stay inside, or did they go outside? Compare your ideas. Then read these sentences about what happened next. Two of them are not right.

1. Everything was fine for the children, for three days.
2. The children stayed inside the house.
3. The wind started blowing.
4. The children were not scared.
5. The children went into the house and locked the doors and windows.
6. Suddenly the rain started and they heard the rain god, Ojumbala.

📖 Listen to the next part of the story and change the sentences that are not right.

Check your answers in groups.
How do you think the story ends? Discuss your guesses.

📖 Read the end of the story on page 66, and listen to it on the recording.

The end of Adesose's story:

Ojumbala came inside the house. He swallowed six children, but the little one crawled under the bed and hid. Ojumbala was so full he could not move. He just sat there.

The old man and the old woman decided to go home. They arrived and called out to the children. Everything was quiet. They opened the door and saw Ojumbala. The mother started to shout. But the father went to the kitchen and got a big knife. He hit Ojumbala and started to squeeze him. The six children came out, one by one. 'Where is the seventh child?' asked the parents. Just then, the little one came out from under the bed. His mother was very pleased and hugged him. These were the luckiest children in the world, because they were saved.

Do you have stories like this one in your country? Tell or mime one to the class.

QC Now do the **Quick Check** exercises your teacher will give you.

C

1 It was a wonderful film | listening; asking questions using the simple past tense |

Listen to your teacher talking about a book or a film. Ask questions about it.

2 When did you see the film?

practice with past tenses; speaking

Match the words and pictures.

    a book   a film   a television set   a radio

Choose two and write down the names.

– a book you read in the last month and liked
– a film you saw and liked
– a programme you heard on the radio and liked
– a programme you saw on TV and liked

Work with a partner. Ask each other these questions.

1. What did you read, see or hear?
2. When did you see it / read it / hear it?
3. What was it about?
4. What did you like about it?

Example: A: *What did you see?*   B: *I saw a film on television.*
          A: *What was it about?*   B: *It was about a young boy and a cinema in Italy.*
          A: *What did you like about it?*   B: *It was funny and sad at the same time. The little boy was great.*

1 ....

2 ....

3 ....

4 ....

Talk with others about what they liked. What books, films or programmes are popular in the class?

3 I just watch the news, that's all

discussion

Which of the programmes do you think are:

– news programmes?
– films?
– programmes for children?
– comedies or amusing programmes?
– documentaries?

With a partner, choose two from the list. Decide which programmes are popular with them.

– ten-year-old children
– teenagers
– elderly people
– your friends
– your teacher
– you

Make a list of some of your favourite TV programmes. Compare with others.

TV and RADIO

(T) Teletext   (R) Repeat   (S) Stereo

Channel 1

4.30	Storytime
5.00	Cartoon: Tim's Day Out
5.15	Newsround
5.30	The Witch Tree
6.00	World News and Weather
6.45	Newsview
7.00	Jenny Martin's Laugh-in
7.30	The Birds of the Serengeti (R) (S)
8.15	Sportsworld: A Ski Jumper's Life
9.00	The World at Nine, News and Sports (T)
9.30	Film on One: The Orient Express (1994) (PG)
11.00	Reviewing the Past: War in the Pacific
12.00	Weather

QC Now do the **Quick Check** exercises your teacher will give you.

PERSONAL STUDY WORKBOOK

- past tenses of irregular verbs
- past tense question forms, positive and negative statements
- pronunciation work
- reading legends from different countries
- completing a factual report
- visual dictionary – the story of a meeting

REVIEW OF UNIT 8

1   I really hate standing in queues | -ing forms; writing |

Complete the sentences with an expression from the box.

I quite like …
I like …
I love …
I really love …
I don't like …
I hate …
I really hate …

> going to parties   having a big breakfast   sleeping with the lights on
> using a computer   reading in a crowded train   cooking a meal
> going to nightclubs   getting presents   standing in queues   travelling
> helping people   working at night   listening to loud music   eating in bed
> using the dictionary   wearing formal clothes   spending money

Find someone in the class with two of the same choices.

Write a paragraph to compare your choices with another person's.

Example: *Li and I hate wearing formal clothes. Li likes working at night, but I don't. I like working in
the morning. I also like spending money, but Li really hates shopping.*

REVIEW OF UNIT 9

1   A hundred years ago, our town was very small | simple past tense; speaking |

Think about your town (or your city or village) a hundred years ago. Answer the
questions. If you don't know, try to guess.

1. Was your town large or small?
2. Did it have many schools? Were they large or small?
3. Did people travel a lot? How did they travel?
4. How did they communicate with each other? Did they send letters?

Use some of these expressions if you like.

> small   dusty   roads not paved   wooden buildings   many churches or mosques
> a few small shops   a big market   a one-room school   used horses
> a horse and cart   donkeys   travelled on foot   sent letters every day
> letters arrived quickly

Compare your ideas with others in the class.

2   Our town was a small village then | listening |

⊂⊃ Listen to two people talking about their town a hundred years ago. Make notes
about what they say.

SPEAKER 1: ....
....
....
....

SPEAKER 2: ....
....
....
....

Are their towns similar to yours?

11

WHAT'S GOING ON?

Language focus:
present continuous for things happening now,
temporary situations and developing situations
contrast present simple and present continuous

Vocabulary:
daily routines and happenings
the quality of life

A

1 What's happening? | present continuous: things happening now |

1 ..... She's calling a taxi.

..... They're having a party.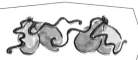

..... She's walking down the street.

..... They're flying to Sydney.

..... They're building a new house.

..... She's using the computer.

..... He's having a shower.

..... He's making a cup of coffee.

..... They're repairing the road.

📼 Listen and number the sentences from 1 to 9. Number 1 is done as an example. Check your answers with others.

2 I'm standing in front of Government House | present continuous; listening; speaking |

Talk about these questions with others.

– Do you often listen to the news? Do you prefer news reports on the radio, on the television, or in the newspapers?
– How important is it for you to hear or read news reports?

📼 Listen to two news reports. Is the situation a, b or c?

1. a. People are walking to the bank to get some money.
   b. People are trying to get more money from the government.
   c. The police are trying to get more money.

2. a. The President and the Prime Minister are arriving in a new country.
   b. The President's leaving the country with her daughter.
   c. The President of one country is meeting a Prime Minister and her husband from another country.

Listen again with a partner. Retell the news reports to each other.

3 I'm learning, but slowly $\boxed{\text{present continuous; conversation}}$

What are you learning at the moment? Complete the sentences in as many different ways as you can.

I'm learning ....

I'm learning to ....

Examples: *I'm learning English at night school.*
I'm learning to cook. My friend's teaching me.

Compare your sentences.

4 In the evenings, I usually watch TV $\boxed{\text{present simple / present continuous; writing}}$

Study these sentences.

A: I **usually** do my shopping on Mondays, but **today** I'm staying at home instead.
B: I live in France but **at the moment** I'm staying with my friend in Bogota.

Write two sentences about yourself (or your family or friends) using the same pattern.

I	usually normally	....	but	at the moment today now just now	I'm	....

My	brother cousin friends	usually	....	but just now	he she they	....

You can use some of these verbs if you like.

I live.	I'm living. (I am living.)
I stay.	I'm staying. (I am staying.)
He does.	He's doing. (He is doing.)
She goes.	She's going. (She is going.)
We take.	We're taking. (We are taking.)
We study.	We're studying. (We are studying.)
They feel.	They're feeling. (They are feeling.)
They work.	They're working. (They are working.)

Read your sentences to the class.

QC Now do the **Quick Check** exercises your teacher will give you.

B

1 I'm having a wonderful time $\boxed{\text{present continuous: temporary/developing situations; listening}}$

Read the notes and check the meaning.

a waiter ......   *a housewife* ......   *a teacher* ......   *a secretary* ......
enjoying a holiday ......   *doing a temporary job* ......   *doing a first job* ......
spending time on the beach ......   *working until late at night* ......
working for a big company ......   *seeing interesting things* ......
learning a language for a holiday ......   *living on a boat* ......

▭▭ ▭▭ Listen to four people. Which person are the notes about? Put 1, 2, 3 or 4 next to each note. Listen again if you like. Compare your answers with others.

2 I'm studying English and really enjoying it

1

Greetings from sunny Thailand! I'm having a wonderful time – seeing a lot of interesting things, spending a lot of time on the beach ... I'm really enjoying the rest!

Lots of love
Kath

2

Dear Meg,
Thanks for your card! Lucky you, travelling all over South America. I'm still here in Manchester with the kids. Still no job, but I'm learning Spanish for our holidays later on this year. It's hard, but a lot of fun – my pronunciation is slowly getting better. Adios and all that,
Mia

3

Dear Feliz,

I'm in Sydney for a year. I'm working for a company to get some experience – and I'm learning a lot! I can't afford a flat so I'm living on a boat for the moment.

Love to all of you,

Dinu

4

Dear Ali,
Did I tell you I got a job in a restaurant here for the summer? I'm enjoying it – lots of free food! – but I'm very tired. I'm on my feet all day! How's your summer? Are you studying hard? Can you come and visit?
See you soon I hope,

Edi

Which writers are:
– doing a temporary job?   ....
– having a holiday?   ....
– at home?   ....
– learning new things?   ....

Choose A or B.

A: Write a postcard to a friend – or to the authors of this book – from your classroom. Use some of the expressions in the box if you like.

B: Imagine a wonderful place to be right now. Write a postcard to people in your class from that place. Use some of the expressions in the box if you like.

> I'm writing to you from the classroom here in ...
> I'm sitting here in ...... and thinking of you.
> The teacher is talking about ...
> I'm staying here with ...
> I'm by myself.
> I'm feeling ...
> I'm finding ...
> I'm learning ...

QC Now do the **Quick Check** exercises your teacher will give you.

C

1 Is the cost of living going up?

present continuous: developing situations; discussion

With a partner, choose one of the three answers.

Talk about your answers. What about: the number of people in your country, the number of cars, the number of tourists? Are they going up or down?

Example: A: *What do you think: is the cost of living going up?*
B: *Well, the government says no, but I'm sure it is going up. What's happening about cars?*
A: *The number of cars is really going up fast. You can't move on the roads now.*

IN OUR COUNTRY:

1 The cost of living is
a. going up.   b. staying the same.   c. going down.

2 Unemployment (people out of work) is
a. going up.   b. staying the same.   c. going down.

3 The number of years people spend in education is
a. going up.   b. staying the same.   c. going down.

4 The level of water pollution is
a. going up.   b. staying the same.   c. going down.

5 The popularity of sports is
a. going up.   b. staying the same.   c. going down.

2 The cost of living is certainly going up!

reading; listening

Three people answered the same questions. Read what they said. Can you guess the missing words?

Jean-Pierre, France

1 In my country, the cost of living is going up. So is unemployment. The number of years that people spend in education is also going .... The level of water pollution is going .... The popularity of sports is going ....

2 The cost of living in my country is certainly going .... and at the same time, unemployment is going .... as well. And that's why many people spend more time in education. So the number of years people spend in education is going .... , because if people face unemployment after school they stay in education as long as they can. Fortunately, the level of water pollution is going ...., and that is because the government is taking steps to reduce the levels of pollution. The popularity of sports? Well, I don't know about that. I think it is ....

Gertrude, Germany

Candy, the United States

3 In my country, the cost of living is going .... , but more slowly than in the past. Unemployment is also going .... , very quickly. The number of years people spend in education is going .... as education becomes more and more important. The level of water pollution is unfortunately going .... , but so is awareness of the problem. That's also going up. The popularity of sports is .... I think. Sports have always been popular, especially football and baseball.

Listen to them answering the questions and check your guesses. Are their ideas about their countries different from yours?

3 Who is spending money on us? [writing]

Read these letters to the editor of a newspaper.

Dear Sir,
I'm tired of this government. Unemployment is going up, and so is the level of pollution. The cost of living is also going up, almost every day. And what is the government doing? It's spending more money on sport! It's spending money on government salaries as well, of course. But what about us? Who is spending money on us? Our school buildings are terrible, our hospitals are full, sometimes we can't drink our water. Please, Madam President, can you do something now? We're waiting for some good news!
Yours faithfully,

Dear Sir,
I'm so happy I'm living in our country now. The government is spending money on education and sports, and they're also building a beautiful new palace for the President. Other countries are seeing the good results of our government's important actions. More tourists are coming as well. This is good for us. We are living in exciting times. Congratulations, Madam President.
Yours faithfully,

Write a letter to an editor. Use some of the expressions in the box.

Exchange your letters with others.

Dear Sir,   Dear Madam,
connecting expressions: also   as well   so is
Yours faithfully,

QC Now do the **Quick Check** exercises your teacher will give you.

PERSONAL STUDY WORKBOOK

- present continuous tense
- contrasting present simple and present continuous
- listening to 'news flashes' from the past
- reading text – a survey of the reading habits of teenagers
- writing short notes, greetings
- visual dictionary – actions

D   REVIEW AND DEVELOPMENT

REVIEW OF UNIT 9

1   I opened the door, then you closed it   [vocabulary building: opposites; past tenses: regular verbs]

What are the opposites of these verbs in the simple past tense? Use a dictionary.

opened – closed	stopped – s _ _ _ _ _ _
departed – a _ _ _ _ _ _	packed – u _ _ _ _ _ _ _
locked – u _ _ _ _ _ _ _	asked – a _ _ _ _ _ _ _
hated – l _ _ _ _	played – w _ _ _ _ _

Make up a story using two of the words from your opposites list (in the past tense) and one of the things in the picture. Mime your story to the class. Answer their questions and then listen to them telling your story.

---

2 Broke, spoke, woke

pronunciation: past tenses – irregular verbs

Write the simple past form of these verbs. (Use a dictionary). Which one in each group doesn't rhyme with the others?

1. break   speak   wake   make
2. ring   sing   bring
3. send   mend   go
4. hide   do   ride
5. watch   catch   buy
6. think   drink   stink
7. sell   tell   spell
8. grin   begin   run

💿 Listen to the past tenses and check your answers. Repeat the verbs.

REVIEW OF UNIT 10

1 The Iceman

reading; listening

Match the words and their definitions.

to survive	to look for a lost person
to rescue someone	an extraordinary event
to search for someone	to stay alive in hard conditions
a miracle	damage to the body caused by extreme cold
frostbite	to find and save a person in trouble

Check your answers with others and talk about this survival problem:

How long can a young person survive with two chocolate bars and only snow to drink in winter in the Himalayas?

Decide on a number of days. Write it on a piece of paper.

Now read an article about James Scott.

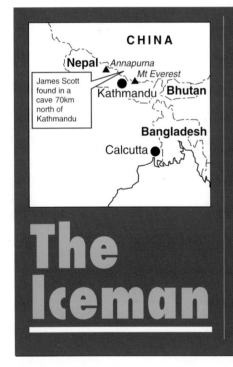

James Scott, a 23-year-old student from Brisbane, has a new name. People call him 'the Iceman'. James survived for a long time in the Himalayas in the middle of winter. He had only light clothes (light shoes, a straw hat, thin trousers and a jacket) and two chocolate bars. Experts believe his strong personality kept him alive. Many people who visited the area thought that his survival was almost a miracle.

Part of the miracle is that rescuers found him at all. He lost contact with the friend he was with, and search teams could not find him. They spent many days looking. His sister made sure that they didn't give up the search.

When the rescue team found him, he was very thin. To stay alive he probably drank snow. Extreme cold usually causes frostbite, but rescuers said that James did not have much frostbite. He went to hospital for a short time only.

Some people think that the story isn't true – especially because James started advertising chocolate bars when he left hospital.

How many days do you think James survived in the Himalayas? Give reasons.

💿 Listen to two people discussing James Scott's story. Answer the questions.

1. How many days did he survive in the snow?
2. How do they think he survived?
3. Do they think the story is true?

What do you think about the story? Do you think it's true? Why or why not?

12

MAKING PLANS

Language focus:
present continuous: future events, already arranged
going to + infinitive: future events,
already arranged / things you intend to do

Vocabulary:
weekend activities, business activities,
language learning activities

A

1 My weekend's always too short | vocabulary; discussion |

Ask another person: How much free time do you get at the weekend?

No free time?   Half a day?   1 day?   2 days?

Here are some words to describe weekends. With a partner write in the opposites.

Example: *short* – **long**

busy – q _ _ _ _
boring – in _ _ _ _ _ _ _ _ _
relaxing – tir _ _ _ *or* ex _ _ _ _ _ _ _ _

Ask and answer questions about your weekend. Use some of the words you wrote.

Examples: A: *Are your weekends usually busy?*
  B: *Yes.*
  A: *Why?*
  B: *Because I work on Saturdays and Sundays. How about you? Are your weekends busy?*
  A: *No, not usually. I like quiet weekends, they're more relaxing.*

2 What are you doing this weekend? | listening |

▭▭ Listen to four people talking. What are they doing this weekend?
Write down their answers.

What are they doing this weekend?

Gill: ....

John: ....

James: ....

Irene: ....

Check your answers with others.

3 What are you doing on Saturday? | present continuous: future events, already arranged |

Ask three other people questions about their plans for the weekend. You can use the
activities in the box to help you.

Examples: *What are you doing this weekend?*
What are you doing on Saturday?
What are you doing on Sunday evening?

Is anyone doing these things this weekend?

- going to a party
- going to the cinema
- going to work
- going for a drive
- making a meal for friends
- going out with children
- visiting relatives or friends
- other activities? ....

Tell other people in the class what you found out. Say two things that are true, and
one thing that is false. Can others guess the false plan?

Example: A: *Maria's going to the cinema on Sunday, Giovanni's staying at home all weekend, and
Tomo's going to Paris.*
B: *I don't think Giovanni's staying at home all weekend. He always goes out.*
A: *Yes, you're right. That's the false one. He's going to a party – as usual!*

QC Now do the **Quick Check** exercises your teacher will give you.

B

1 I write down all my meetings in my diary | conversation |

Talk about these questions with
others.

- How do you plan your work?
  Do you use a diary, a wall
  chart, your computer? Other
  ways?
- Is it difficult to plan your week?
  Why or why not? Is your week
  busy or quiet, interesting or
  boring?
- Do you have any appointments?
- Do you go to any meetings?

2 I'm sorry she can't see you   present continuous; reading; answering questions

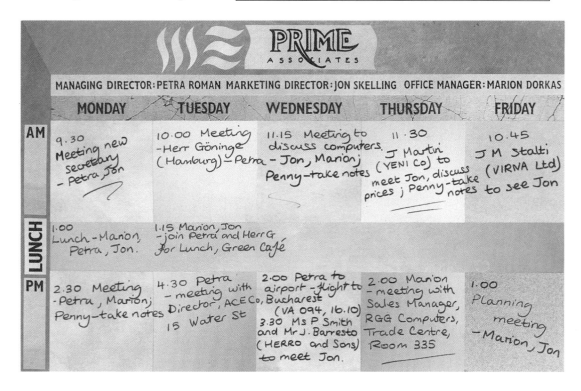

PRIME ASSOCIATES

MANAGING DIRECTOR: PETRA ROMAN   MARKETING DIRECTOR: JON SKELLING   OFFICE MANAGER: MARION DORKAS

	MONDAY	TUESDAY	WEDNESDAY	THURSDAY	FRIDAY
AM	9.30 Meeting new secretary – Petra, Jon	10.00 Meeting – Herr Göninge (Hamburg) – Petra	11.15 Meeting to discuss computers. – Jon, Marion; Penny – take notes	11.30 J Martin (YENI Co) to meet Jon, discuss prices; Penny – take notes	10.45 J M Stalti (VIRNA Ltd) to see Jon
LUNCH	1.00 Lunch – Marion, Petra, Jon.	1.15 Marion, Jon – join Petra and Herr G for Lunch, Green Café			
PM	2.30 Meeting – Petra, Marion; Penny – take notes	4.30 Petra – meeting with Director, ACE Co, 15 Water St	2.00 Petra to airport – flight to Bucharest (VA 094, 16.10) 3.30 Ms P Smith and Mr J. Barresto (HERRO and Sons) to meet Jon.	2.00 Marion – meeting with Sales Manager, RGG Computers, Trade Centre, Room 335	1.00 Planning meeting – Marion, Jon

Read this weekly diary for a small company. Help each other with any difficulties.

Imagine that you are the receptionist. You are going to receive some phone calls. Read the questions and prepare answers for them.

Example:

Question on the recording: *Can Mr Skelling see some clients at 9.30 on Monday?*

Possible answer: *No, I'm sorry he can't. He's meeting the new secretary.*

> **HELP**
>
> Let me check.
> I'm sorry, she can't.
> I'm terribly sorry, but she's not free.
> I'm afraid she's going away that day.
> Yes, that seems fine.

Phone call 1: Can Mrs Roman go to a meeting at 3 pm on Wednesday?

Phone call 2: Hello, this is Mr Brown's secretary. Can either Petra or Marion see Mr Brown at 10 am on Tuesday?

Phone call 3: This is John Peters speaking. I'm coming to the city on Friday and I'd like to meet Marion Dorkas at 9.30 in the morning. Is she free at that time?

Phone call 4: Hello, there, Guy here. Can you tell me: are Marion and Jon free for lunch on Monday?

Phone call 5: Hello, Herr Göninge's office here. Herr Göninge's having some trouble with his travel plans. Could he change his meeting with Mrs Roman from Tuesday morning to Monday morning, at the same time?

Phone call 6: Hello, it's Keith here. Is Jon busy at 11 on Friday morning?

Phone call 7: Can Marion come to a meeting on Thursday afternoon?

⌕ Now listen to the questions on the recording and answer them.

3 Next Thursday, I'm meeting the new students   asking questions about plans

Write next week's diary for your teacher. Ask questions and fill in planned events.

Example: *What are you doing on Monday evening?*
Are you doing anything on Tuesday morning?

QC Now do the **Quick Check** exercises your teacher will give you.

C

1 I'm going to read a newspaper every day! [*going to* + infinitive; reading]

Read this letter to a class of English learners. The writer left and moved to Canada. Try to remember the things she is going to do to improve her English.

> Dear English class,
>
> I arrived in Canada a week ago and already I think that my English is improving! I'm living in a small flat near the centre of Toronto. It's cheap and quite comfortable.
>
> In your letter you ask what I'm going to do to improve my English. Well, tomorrow I'm going to visit the university to see what English courses they offer there in the evenings. Of course, I'm going to read a newspaper every day. I'm also going to try to get a part-time job because then I can speak English a lot more. I'm going to spend a lot on cassettes because listening is so important! There are some good bookshops here, so I'm also going to look for some other books to use by myself. Can you recommend anything? I'm going to write a diary in English – that's a good way to learn English.
>
> How are you getting on? I was sorry I had to leave in the middle of the course. Are you going to write to me again?
> Hope to hear from you all soon,
> Olga

Without looking at the book, list what Olga is going to do to improve her English. Work with a partner.

She's going to …

2 She's going to get a part-time job [listening]

⊂⊃ Listen to the recording. There are four differences in the things the writer is going to do. What are they? Write them down.

Compare with a partner.

3 My learning resolutions [present simple and *going to* + infinitive; writing; conversation]

What do you do to improve your English? Tick any things on the list that you do, and add others.

	sometimes	often	every day
I read my English book at home.		✓	
I listen to the cassettes at home.	✗		
I come to class.		✗	
I read English newspapers and magazines.	✗		
I talk to English speakers outside class.		✗	
I use English on the phone.		✗	
I watch films or videos in English.		✗	
I listen to English on the radio.	✗		
I study grammar books.	✗		
I keep a vocabulary book.	✗		
I write a diary in English.	✗		
I use my dictionary a lot.	✗		
I			
I			

Now make two lists. Write down the things you are going to do and not going to do to improve your English after this course.

I'm going to …   *I'm not going to …*

....

....

....

Talk about your lists with a partner.

Examples: A: *What do you do to improve your English?*
B: *I read the newspaper every day and I sometimes listen to cassettes.*
A: *What are you going to do after this course?*
B: *I'm going to keep a diary in English, but I'm not going to study grammar books.*

QC Now do the **Quick Check** exercises your teacher will give you.

PERSONAL STUDY WORKBOOK

• present continuous for pre-arranged plans
• *going to* future for general intentions
• pronunciation practice: /ŋ/
• reading text – an article about holiday plans
• writing a short paragraph about yourself
• visual dictionary – future plans and leisure activities

D REVIEW AND DEVELOPMENT

REVIEW OF UNIT 10

1 They found both alligators in bed | reading; past tenses |

Read the two news articles. Complete them, using the verbs in the boxes.

No alligators in bed!

John M Butler had two 1.2-metre alligators as pets. For 23 months, he .... for official permission to keep them in his motorhome. He applied in November 1989 for a permit. The officers finally went to his motorhome in Miami, Florida in October 1991 to make sure it was big enough for alligators.

When the officers ...., they .... both alligators in Mr Butler's bed. Mr Butler .... at the hospital getting treatment for alligator bites. The officers .... away the alligators, and .... to give him official permission to keep them. Mr Butler later complained. He .... it was wrong to take away his property without his permission.

| arrived | asked | was | found | said | took | refused |

No live worms for lunch!

On Friday, a group of animal lovers .... that eating live worms was terrible. David Diamond, 53, ... the worms, in a pub, to get money for a new hospital. The worms .... from his own garden.

'Worms are not as bad as people think', Diamond said. 'They .... just like spaghetti. A quick bite, and they soon .... wriggling,' he .... the local newspaper. He said that eating worms was not so terrible and that officers of the British Army also ate them.

stopped   came   told   were   ate   said

2 The police caught him   writing a short news article

Write a short news article like the ones in Exercise 1. Think of an event in your town or city – or look at the pictures and imagine what happened.

Read your article to the class, or display it.

REVIEW OF UNIT 11

1 A special memory   vocabulary and discussion

How do you save special memories?

photographs   diaries   letters   newspaper articles

What do you like – or what don't you like – about these ways of saving memories?

Examples: *I like photographs because they remind me of places.*
I don't like newspaper articles because I always lose them.

2 What are you doing?   listening; writing down notes; speaking

⫘ Listen to the recording and write down notes.

Work with a partner. Compare your notes and tell each other about your memories.

13

BETTER AND BETTER

Language focus:	Vocabulary:
comparative and superlative adjectives	features of countries and cities

A

1 Is Greenland bigger than Australia?

comparative adjectives; listening

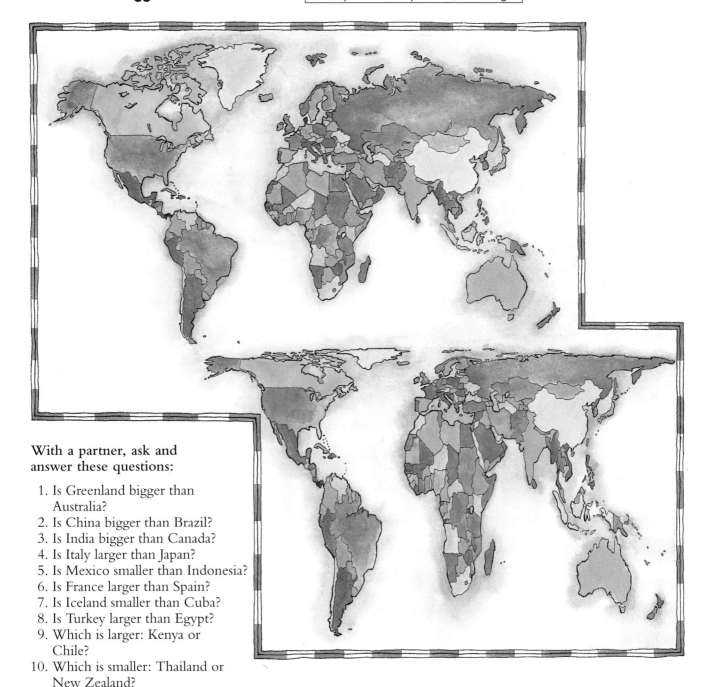

With a partner, ask and answer these questions:

1. Is Greenland bigger than Australia?
2. Is China bigger than Brazil?
3. Is India bigger than Canada?
4. Is Italy larger than Japan?
5. Is Mexico smaller than Indonesia?
6. Is France larger than Spain?
7. Is Iceland smaller than Cuba?
8. Is Turkey larger than Egypt?
9. Which is larger: Kenya or Chile?
10. Which is smaller: Thailand or New Zealand?

Listen to some people answering the questions, and check your answers.

2 It's a bit smaller than ...

comparative adjectives and modifiers

a lot/much smaller   a bit smaller   big/large   a bit bigger/larger   a lot/much bigger/larger

You are going to listen to a recording about three countries. Work in groups of three. Each of you: listen and take notes on a different country. Compare notes with your partners. Try to guess the three countries.

Learner A: Country 1 is:

a lot bigger than ....

a bit smaller than ....

much bigger than ....

Other information: ....

Learner B: Country 2 is:

much smaller than ....

a bit bigger than ....

a bit smaller than ....

Other information: ....

Learner C: Country 3 is:

much, much bigger than ....

a bit smaller than ....

a bit larger than ....

a lot larger than ....

Other information: ....

3 It's much, much bigger than Belgium

writing and guessing

Choose a country. Write a paragraph about it, similar to the ones you listened to.

Example: *The country I chose is a bit smaller than ..., etc.*

Read your paragraph and ask others to guess your country.

QC Now do the **Quick Check** exercises your teacher will give you.

B

1 I like living in the city centre

vocabulary and speaking; comparatives using *more* and *less*

city centre   suburbs   small town   countryside   coast

Look at the picture. Where do you live? In the city? In the suburbs? In the countryside? Near the coast? Where do other members of your family live?

Choose an appropriate place in the picture for each of the words in the box.

| cheap | crowded | clean · | safe | lively | polluted | noisy | dirty | nice |

Compare your choices. Where is a good place to live? Explain your reasons.

Example: A: *I think the countryside is a good place to live. It's much safer than the city.*
   B: *Really? I like living in the city centre. It's more crowded and more polluted, but it's livelier.*

2 Tales of two cities

What do you know about Istanbul in Turkey, and Brasilia in Brazil? Compare your ideas with others.

Guess which statements are about Brasilia, and which are about Istanbul. Use a dictionary to help you.

1. It's very polluted.
2. It's very tidy.
3. Hotels are all together in one part of the city, banks in another part and schools in another.
4. There are many people shouting as they sell things in the streets.
5. You can't see shops because they are inside large buildings.
6. It is a place full of contrasts.
7. There is an exciting underground cathedral.
8. There is a lot of space around the buildings.
9. There is a lot of noise inside the covered bazaar.
10. At busy times of the day, the traffic is terrifying.

Read these articles about the two cities and check your answers.

① *Brasilia – a new city*

BRASILIA is different from many cities, because it is a planned city. It's very tidy: there are no television aerials, no lines of washing hanging out to dry, no advertising. There are not many smells, and not much noise except for the traffic on the motorway.

Buildings of different types are not in the same place. Hotels are all together in one part of the city, banks in another part, and schools in another. From the outside, you can't see any shops – they are inside large buildings.

People live in flats in buildings that have either two or six floors. All the buildings have a lot of space around them, and some are very impressive. For example, there is an exciting underground cathedral. The Foreign Ministry is surrounded by water.

There is no overcrowding, there are no traffic problems. But is there simply too much space? Is everything so large that it is a bit impersonal? Where are the people? Where is the sound of voices and laughter?

② *Istanbul – an old city*

ISTANBUL is beautiful to look at and great fun. It is noisy, with many people shouting as they sell things in the streets. Istanbul people love flowers and are very friendly toward visitors.

Istanbul is a place full of contrasts, a mixture of old and new. There are lovely, quiet palaces and museums but there's a lot of noise inside the famous Covered Bazaar and in the tiny, crowded, busy alleys such as Flower Sellers' Alley.

The rush-hour traffic can be terrifying. Like so many modern cities, Istanbul is very polluted and has a lot of traffic problems. It is certainly a dirty city, but beautiful at the same time. When you look across the bridge to old Stamboul, you see an extraordinary skyline with mosques and minarets, and you know you are standing, in fact, at the doorway to Asia. Things are happening, and the atmosphere is very exciting.

Study the examples, then answer the questions.

Examples: *Are both cities big?* (both cities = Istanbul and Brasilia)
Yes, they are.
Are both cities modern?
No, they aren't, really. Brasilia is modern, but Istanbul is a mixture of old and new.

1. Are both cities planned?
2. Are there interesting buildings in both cities?
3. Are both cities impersonal?
4. Are both cities tidy?

5. Are both cities quiet?
6. Is traffic a problem in both cities?
7. Are both cities great fun?
8. Are both cities extraordinary?

Which city do you think is:

– more interesting?
– more modern?
– more efficient?
– more beautiful?

– less polluted?
– less varied?
– less crowded?
– less noisy?

Compare your ideas with others.

3 My city's not as old as Istanbul | comparison with negative form; listening; writing |

Listen to seven questions and write down your answers.

Example: 1. You hear the question: *Is your city older than Brasilia?*
You write: *Yes, it's (much) older.* or *No, it's not as old as Brasilia.*
2. You hear the question: *Is your city more interesting than Istanbul?*
You write: *Yes, it's more interesting.* or *No, it's not as interesting as Istanbul.*

Compare your answers with others. Write three or four questions, like the ones you heard. Ask others your questions.

QC Now do the **Quick Check** exercises your teacher will give you.

C

1 The nicest and most interesting cafés are not always the cheapest | superlatives |

Dino's
The cheapest coffee, the finest cakes, the best music – Dino's is the most relaxing spot in town.
Coffee – $1
Special coffee and cake – $2.50

Expresso BAR
The cheapest and the best!
Best expresso coffee – $3.00
Expresso and cake – $5.50

The Coffee Corner
CHEAPEST, QUICKEST, NICEST IN TOWN!
Fresh coffee – $1.50
Try a cream cake with your coffee, only $3.50

True or false? Write *T* or *F*.

1. Dino's is cheaper than the Coffee Corner. ....
2. The Expresso Bar is more expensive than the Coffee Corner. ....
3. The Coffee Corner is cheaper than the Expresso Bar. ....
4. The Expresso Bar has the cheapest coffee. ....
5. The Coffee Corner has the most expensive coffee and cake. ....
6. Dino's has the cheapest coffee. ....

Write *cheaper* or *cheapest* under the coffee cup from Dino's in these pictures.

....

Can you complete the table?

Check your answers with others.

Adjective	Comparative adjective	Superlative adjective
cheap	cheaper	cheapest
nice	....	nicest
quick	quicker	....
fine	....	....
expensive	more expensive	most expensive
relaxing	more relaxing	....
....	better	best
bad	worse	worst

2   The best place for a cup of coffee | writing with superlatives |

A teacher at a language school asks you to prepare a simple list to give to visitors to the town where you are living. Design and write the list. You can use some of these ideas if you like.

Put your lists together and make one class list with all the best ideas.

A LIST FOR VISITORS

Where to eat:
Best place for a cup of good, cheap coffee
Best local food
Cheapest snack bar

Where to stay:
Best hotel for visitors
Cheapest clean place to stay

Things to do and see:
Best places to meet people
Best music
Cheapest or best cinema
Most interesting evening out
Most peaceful place to sit
Most exciting place to visit

Shopping, travel:
Best places to shop
Best way to travel round the town
Best travel agent

Things not to do:
Most dangerous place for tourists
Most dangerous nightclub
Most boring tourist spot
Worst place to eat
Worst place to stay
Worst place to visit

3 Host families   comparatives and superlatives

Is this a good idea for your family? Why or why not? Discuss your opinions with a partner.

Write answers to the questions in the box below. Then interview your partner to find out their answers.

ARE YOU INTERESTED IN OTHER COUNTRIES AND CULTURES?

Can your family host an exchange student for a month or more? Let someone from another country become part of your family and help international understanding.

Phone Jenny at
Western Cross Cultural Exchange
for more details.
Phone 081 939 1183

INTERESTED IN AN EXCHANGE STUDENT? TELL US ABOUT YOUR FAMILY

Western Cross Cultural Exchange

1. How many adults and how many children are there in your home?
.... adults; .... children

2. Which month is a good one for a visitor from another country to stay in your home? ....

3. Which sort of visitor is better for your home?
a) a teenager   b) an adult

4. Which is the best way to get to the city centre from your home?
a) bus   b) train   c) bicycle   d) other ....

5. In which cultures are you and your family most interested?
a) European   b) South American   c) Asian   d) African
e) North American   f) Middle Eastern

6. What is the best word to describe life in your family? ....

7. Which is worse, in your view?
a) a guest who smokes *or*   b) a guest who uses your phone a lot?

8. What do you think is the worst thing about life in your home for a visitor?
a) the noise   b) the cold   c) there isn't much space
d) the dog   e) ....

Join another pair and discuss your answers. Together, prepare a short paragraph about this question.

What sort of families make the best host families?

Read out your paragraphs to the class.

QC Now do the **Quick Check** exercises your teacher will give you.

PERSONAL STUDY WORKBOOK

- comparatives and superlatives
- reading about English sayings
- writing comparisons
- visual dictionary – countries and capitals

REVIEW OF UNIT 11

1 Away from home | role play |

Divide into two groups.

Group A:
You are parents. Your child is in a new situation away from home. Think of questions to ask your child about the new situation. Example: *Are you eating enough? Are you working hard?* Make a list of at least five questions. Use some of the words in the box below.

Group B:
You are young people. You are away from home for the first time at college or in a job. You are now living on your own. You know your parents are worrying about you. Think of things to say to them. Make a list of at least five things to say. Use some of the words in the box below.

| feel | work | sleep | eat | clean | begin |
| fit in | live | fill | slip | play | enjoy | do | keep |

Role play: work with a partner from the other group. Ask and answer the questions you prepared about the situation.

Example: A: *Are you eating enough?*
          B: *Yes, of course I'm eating enough – and I'm learning to cook some really nice things.*

2 Short or long sound? | pronunciation /ɪ/ and /iː/; dictation |

🎧 Listen to ten questions from a parent. After each question, show the sound in the verb you hear. Clap once if it is /ɪ/; clap twice if it is /iː/.

Listen to five of the questions again. Write down each sentence. Compare with a partner.

REVIEW OF UNIT 12

1 What are you doing this evening? | present continuous; pronunciation |

Look at this conversation. With a partner complete the missing questions.

Example: A: *What are you doing this evening?*   B: *I'm going to the cinema.*

A: Who ....?   B: With Midori.

A: What ....?   B: After that? We're having a meal in town.

A: Are you ....?   B: No, we're going in my car.

A: What ....?   B: On Sunday? Nothing, I'm staying at home.

A: When ....?   B: She's arriving on Monday. My father telephoned after she left Singapore.

🎧 Listen to the conversation. Compare the questions with the ones you wrote. Listen again and repeat the questions.

2 What are you doing after class? | conversation |

Choose one of the three questions. Ask two other people your question.

1. What are you doing this evening?
2. What are you doing on Sunday?
3. What are you doing after class?

Tell the class the replies you heard.

Example: *This evening Jamal is helping his father at the shop, and Helena is going to the cinema.*

14

A SPIRIT OF ADVENTURE

Language focus:
present perfect: with *ever* and *never* for
unfinished time with *this week/month/year*
contrast present perfect with simple past

Vocabulary:
sporting activities
illness
stress and relaxation
— learning English

A

1 The first time was really fantastic   vocabulary and listening

Listen to someone talking about an exciting moment. Which picture is she describing?

Water skiing

Camel racing

Hot air ballooning

Scuba diving

Skydiving

Listen to more of her story. Were you right? How did she feel?

2 I love excitement | present perfect with *ever/never*; listening |

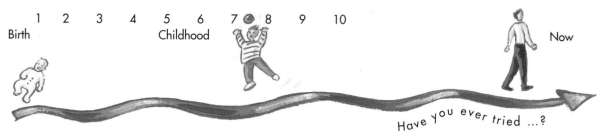

Have you ever tried any of these sports?

	Yes, I've tried it once.	*I've done it lots of times.*	*No, never!*
motor racing	......	......	......
water skiing	......	......	......
horse riding	......	......	......
scuba diving	......	......	......
skydiving	......	......	......
karate	......	......	......
hot air ballooning	......	......	......
hang gliding	......	......	......
sailing	......	......	......

Compare your experiences and your reactions to these sports with a partner.

Example: A: *Have you ever tried motor racing, Kurt?*
B: *Yes, I've tried it once.*

□□ □□ Listen to a man and a woman talking about the sports. Make notes about the sports they have tried and those they haven't tried.

3 Once was enough! | contrasting the past simple and the present perfect; writing |

Study this example from the listening.

Example: A: *What about horse riding?* **Have you ever tried** *that?*
B: *Er … Yes,* **I have.** *I tried it once when I was ten.*

A sports magazine is asking readers to tell them about a) a sport or other activity that they tried once only or b) a sport or activity that they watched once only.

Choose one option, answer the questions and then write the paragraph for the sports magazine. Begin your paragraph *Yes, I have tried …* or *Yes, I have watched … .*

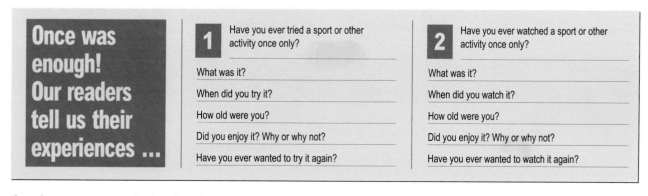

Once was enough! Our readers tell us their experiences …

1 Have you ever tried a sport or other activity once only?

What was it?

When did you try it?

How old were you?

Did you enjoy it? Why or why not?

Have you ever wanted to try it again?

2 Have you ever watched a sport or other activity once only?

What was it?

When did you watch it?

How old were you?

Did you enjoy it? Why or why not?

Have you ever wanted to watch it again?

Read your paragraphs to the class.

QC Now do the **Quick Check** exercises your teacher will give you.

B

1 Fit for life? | vocabulary |

Work with a partner. Use a dictionary. Put the expressions in the box into two lists, under these headings:

Sport   *Health problems*

> stressed   a cold   volleyball   a cough   skiing   a stomachache   tired
> soccer   sore feet   golf   a sore throat   swimming   a broken arm   sailing
> riding   a headache   a bad back   tennis   a broken leg

Which of the expressions go with which verbs? Complete the table.

to have …	*to feel …*	*to play …*	*to go …*
a sore throat	tired	tennis	swimming

Check your answers with others.

2 Have you had a sore throat this year? | present perfect with *this week/month/year* |

Ask a partner ten questions. Find out:

1. Are they active? (5 questions)
2. Are they healthy? (5 questions)

Use some of the expressions from Exercise 1.

Examples:

1. *Have you played tennis this week/month/year?*
2. *Have you had a sore throat this week/month/year?*

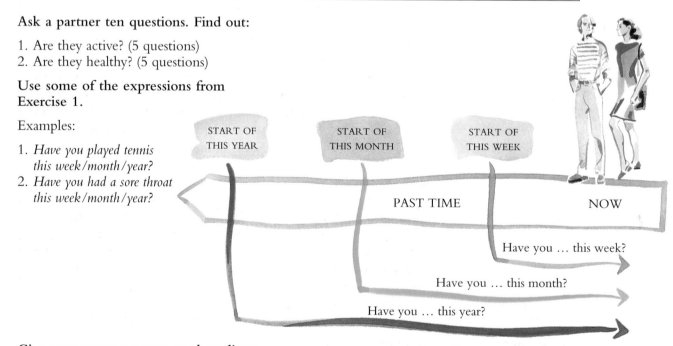

START OF THIS YEAR   START OF THIS MONTH   START OF THIS WEEK

PAST TIME   NOW

Have you … this week?
Have you … this month?
Have you … this year?

Give your partner scores on these lines:

active? (very active) 1 _____ 5 (not very active)
healthy? (very good health) 1 _____ 5 (not very good health)

In small groups, compare scores. Is a healthy person always an active person?

3 Reflexology | reading; discussion |

Study the illustrations with a partner. Have you ever seen this sort of picture before?

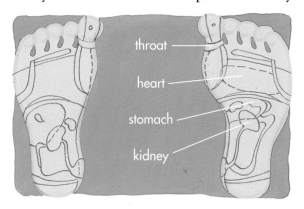

throat

heart

stomach

kidney

Look at these notes from a text on reflexology. Guess what the questions are.

– What is ....?
  a type of massage / uses the pressure points on hands and feet
– When did ....?
  about 4000 BC
– What do ....?
  they believe there are points on hands and feet connecting to the body
– How does ....?
  nobody knows, but perhaps helps energy to move / reduces pain

Read the text, then check your questions with a partner.

Reflexology started thousands of years ago, perhaps as early as 4000 BC. Certainly the Egyptians used it in 2300 BC.

In modern times, American doctors in particular have been interested in reflexology and have used it to treat sports injuries. Dr William Fitzgerald, for example, developed 'zone therapy' in 1917. He divided the body into zones of energy and massaged his patients' fingers to reduce pain. More recently, other American doctors have found that the feet are more responsive to pressure than the hands and so feet have become the most important part of treatment.

Reflexologists believe that there are points (reflexes) on the feet and hands that connect to each part of the body. By massaging these reflexes the reflexologist helps people to feel less tension in their body.

How does reflexology work? Nobody knows exactly, but some believe it helps energy to move in the body and unblocks tension or other energy blocks in the body. Treatment usually takes about 30–40 minutes and at the end of treatment the main feeling is one of relaxation.

Touch is very important in reflexology. The reflexologist uses fingers and thumbs to work on the reflexes. Touch is the first sense to develop in babies. It gives comfort and warmth. To touch someone is to value them. In fact touch is the language of massage, both Eastern and Western.

In groups, discuss your views on reflexology. Report your views to another group.

– Is reflexology popular in your country?   – Have you ever had a foot massage?
– Is it helpful, do you think?   – Have you tried reflexology recently?

QC Now do the **Quick Check** exercises your teacher will give you.

C

1 Is your English in good shape? | present perfect: negative forms |

Think of your recent experiences of learning English. Tick any statement which is true for you. Write others. Compare your answers with a partner.

...... I've learned a lot of new words.
...... I've enjoyed meeting people in class.
...... I've tried to read English newspapers.

...... I've worked hard and have made good progress.
...... I've tried hard but progress is slow.
...... I haven't enjoyed studying at home much.

2 Personal progress | writing |

Complete this report on your progress. Discuss your scores with a partner.

Personal Progress

I've now had .... weeks (months) of English, about .... hours altogether. This month, I have made (slow/satisfactory/good/very good) progress. I have enjoyed .... , but I haven't found it easy to ....

These are my personal scores for the following:

Effort ....../10
Studying outside of class ....../10
Enjoyment ....../10
Developing my own ways of learning English ....../10

My progress with these:

Listening to English ....../10
Speaking English ....../10
Reading English ....../10
Learning vocabulary ....../10
Writing in English ....../10
Pronunciation ....../10

3 A journal entry | reading; writing |

Read this monthly journal by an English person who is learning Japanese.

This month, I've found it quite easy to speak Japanese and I can now have simple conversations about shopping, my family and my job. I've learned a lot of vocabulary. I've enjoyed being in a class with other learners because we try to talk together in Japanese. I've also tried to study at home for about half an hour a day. I've watched one or two Japanese films but I didn't understand much. I haven't found it easy to learn Japanese writing, and I can't read much in Japanese except numbers and days. I've had difficulty with word order in Japanese because it is so different from English. I'm quite pleased with my progress but I haven't got time for classes next month. I'm going to work with my book at home. I hope I can remember what I've learned.

Write a journal entry for *your* learning of English this month.

QC Now do the **Quick Check** exercises your teacher will give you.

PERSONAL STUDY WORKBOOK

- present perfect
- reading a learner's progress report
- writing a progress report and a postcard
- listening to people talking about sports
- pronunciation work
- visual dictionary – sport

REVIEW OF UNIT 12

1 Guessing game | *going to* for things you intend to do; writing; discussion |

What interesting things are you going to do this week?
Write down three things.

In small groups, try to guess what others are going to do.

Examples: A: *I think you're going to buy a present.*
B: *No, I'm not.*
A: *You're going to meet a friend and go to a restaurant for lunch.*
B: *That's right. You've guessed it. Now what about you ….
Are you going to pay your phone bill?*
A: *No, I haven't got a phone in my flat.*

*This week I'm going to
buy ....
pay ....
go to ....*

In your group, write a note about someone's intentions.

Example: *This week, X is going to buy a new pair of shoes. X is
also going to go to meet a friend in Paris. Because of that,
X is not going to come to our next class.*

Read out the notes to other groups. Can they guess X's name?

REVIEW OF UNIT 13

1 The easiest pet to keep is a fish | practice with superlatives |

Answer these questions.

As a pet, which animal …
– is the easiest to keep?
– is the most expensive to keep?
– is the quietest?
– is the friendliest?
– is the most dangerous?
– is the most intelligent?
– has the longest life?
– is the most endangered as a species?

– is the most trouble to keep?
– is the least expensive to keep?
– is the noisiest?
– is the least friendly?
– is the least dangerous?
– is the least intelligent
– has the shortest life?

Compare your answers with a partner.

2 They're pretty independent | listening |

Listen to some people answering some of the questions in Exercise 1. Here are
some notes. Complete the missing parts.

Question?	Animal	Reason(s)
1. easiest to keep?	....	only need a bit of food each day, independent
2.	....	large brain
3.	parrot	....
4.	....	barks a lot

Check your answers with others in the class.

15

DOES BEING TIDY SAVE TIME?

Language focus:	Vocabulary:
-ing forms	everyday activities
	offices, managing information, computers

A

1 I'm very absent-minded | vocabulary and speaking |

Put a cross on the line to show what kind of person you are:

I'm very absent-minded;
I keep losing things.

I'm well-organised;
I don't forget things.

Compare your line with others. Who are the absent-minded people in your class?

2 Ever? Sometimes? All the time? | contrast of verb forms; writing questions |

Put in the missing verbs.
Add one more verb.

Have you ever ...?	*Do you sometimes ...?*	*Do you keep ...ing?*
lost	lose	losing
left	....	leaving
....	forget	forgetting
....	....	putting
....	....	locking
....	....	....

Write six questions. Use two verb forms from each list.

Examples: *Do you keep forgetting to pay for things?*
             Have you ever lost an important letter?
             Do you sometimes forget your glasses?

3 No, I've never forgotten anyone's birthday!

answering questions; listening

Think of ways of answering your six questions. Put a tick next to any of these statements that you think is right.

☐ 1. You can answer *Have you ever ...?* questions with:
Yes, I have or *No, I haven't* or *Yes, once* or *No, never.*
☐ 2. You can answer *Have you ever ...?* questions with:
Yes, I do or *No, I don't.*
☐ 3. You can answer *Do you keep ...ing?* questions with:
Yes, I have, once or *No, I haven't.*
☐ 4. You can answer *Do you keep ...ing?* questions with:
Yes, I do or *No, I don't.*
☐ 5. You can answer *Do you sometimes ...?* questions with:
Yes, I've sometimes ... or *No, I've never ... .*
☐ 6. You can answer *Do you sometimes ...?* questions with:
Yes, I do or *No, never.*

Check your answers. Work with a partner. Ask each other your questions, and answer them appropriately.

▭ Listen to six answers to questions like the ones you have written. Complete the questions.

Questions:
a. Have .... your passport?
b. .... in the evenings?
c. .... keep losing ....?
d. .... breaking things?
e. .... car keys in the car?
f. .... your wife's ....?

Listen again. This time you can hear the questions and compare them with yours.

QC Now do the **Quick Check** exercises your teacher will give you.

B

1 Before going home, I always tidy my desk

before and *after* + *-ing* form; speaking

In small groups, compare your reactions to these questions.

Is the place where you work tidy? Or is it usually untidy?
Do you keep pens and pencils in a box?
Do you tidy your desk after opening letters?
Do you put your cup away after having some coffee?
Do you put books and dictionaries away after using them?
Do you always file pieces of paper after reading them?
Do you make a list of things to do before starting to work in the morning?
Do you tidy your desk at work before leaving or at home before going to bed?
Do you always finish one thing before starting another?

Are most people in your class tidy or untidy workers?

2 It's time to tackle the memo mountain   reading

Take a guess and fill in the spaces with a number. Then compare your guesses with others.

1. The average office worker looks for things on or around the desk for .... minutes a day.
2. Office workers look at each piece of paper up to .... times a day.
3. Worldwide, computer printers print out .... pieces of paper every minute.
4. Worldwide, photocopiers copy .... sheets of paper an hour.

Read this article and see how good your guesses were. Help each other with any difficulties.

Time to tackle the memo mountain

Today is International Clear your Desk Day, and 250,000 British office workers are throwing out old memos and faxes. All over Britain, workers are tidying their desks, according to management consultant Declan Treacy, head of the Clear Your Desk! organisation. His job is to visit companies and tell them how to manage their paperwork.

Mr Treacy says we spend 45 minutes a day just looking for things on and around our desks, and we look at each piece of paper up to five times a day. He says that all over the world, computer printers produce 2.5 million pieces of paper every minute and photocopiers copy 60 million sheets of paper an hour. Untidy desks, says Mr Treacy, lead to lost information and high stress.

Mr Treacy says two hours is enough to clear a desk. 'There are only four things you can do with a piece of paper that is on your desk – act on it, pass it to another person, file it or put it in the bin.' In his opinion, the best thing to do, after looking at each piece of paper, is to act on it.

But is Mr Treacy right? In our office, we don't file important memos or letters from customers. We think of other useful purposes for them ...

By yourself or with a partner, find parts of the text which are similar in meaning to these sentences:

Example: Sentence: *He explains to company workers how they can deal with all the paper that comes into their offices.*
In the text: *His job is to visit companies and tell them how to manage their paperwork.*

1. When people do not keep their desks tidy, they lose some facts they need.
2. In Mr Treacy's opinion, you only need a couple of hours to tidy your desk.
3. After studying a piece of paper, it's a good idea to do something with it.
4. Office workers are stressed because their workplace is untidy.

Do you agree with Mr Treacy's opinions on what to do with pieces of paper?

3 Other useful purposes | -ing forms after *for*; writing |

Look again at the end of the text in Exercise 2.

In our office, we don't file important memos or letters from customers. We think of other useful purposes for them ...

Complete the sentences. Use your own endings, or an appropriate ending from the box. Add one more sentence.

Letters from customers are useful for ....

Old envelopes are handy for ....

We don't throw away old postcards. They are good for ....

Old newspapers are good for ....

.... are useful for ....

> putting under one leg of an old chair   killing flies   making paper airplanes   lighting fires
> writing down telephone numbers   wrapping around sandwiches   making hats when it rains

Read your sentences to others.

QC Now do the **Quick Check** exercises your teacher will give you.

C

1 Managing information is useful | -ing form as subject |

People manage information in many different ways today. Choose words from the box to complete the table. Use a dictionary. Some words can go in both columns.

> filing cabinets   fax   notebooks   compact discs   computers

Managing information in the past	*Managing information today*
Remembering things	Sending a ....
Writing things down	Storing information on ....
Putting information in	Putting information on ....
Keeping record cards (e.g. in libraries)	Keeping records in ....
Keeping records in	....
....	....
....	....

Share your ideas with others in the class. Can you add to the lists?

2 Writing things is not very useful | writing with *-ing* forms |

Look again at your lists. Write statements about some of them. Write each statement with an *-ing* word.

Examples: ***Writing*** *information down helps me to remember it.*
           Keeping *records in computers is easy and fast.*
           Writing *things down is not very useful because it takes a long time.*

Read your statements to a partner. Are they similar? Do you agree?

3 Using computers | speaking; listening |

Many people use computers these days to store information. Answer these questions and then talk about them with others in your class.

– How much do you use computers?
– What do you think they are useful for?
– Are there disadvantages in using computers?

⬤⬤ ⬤⬤ Listen to some people talking about computers. Complete the table.

Good things about computers	Bad things about computers
good for storing addresses	bad for your back
....	....
....	....
....	....
....	....

Do you agree with the speakers? What about learning a language by computer? Do you think it's a good idea?

QC Now do the **Quick Check** exercises your teacher will give you.

PERSONAL STUDY WORKBOOK

- *-ing* forms
- reading about information overload
- writing short comments about work
- visual dictionary – offices

D REVIEW AND DEVELOPMENT

REVIEW OF UNIT 13

1 The best shops are in the market | role play |

Imagine you meet an English-speaking tourist in your home town. This person asks you these questions. Give answers.
A: Ask the questions.
B: Answer them. Then change roles. Ask and answer one more question of your own.

> The best place is …
> The best place is … but …
> The best shops are …
> The most interesting buildings are probably the …
> The best place to ask is …

> I haven't got much money. Where can I stay for the night?
> I've got no money but I have my guitar. Where's the best place for me to play in the street?
> My plane leaves today. Where's the best place to buy some nice souvenirs?
> I'm really interested in old buildings. Which are the most interesting ones?
> I've got no money. Can I get a job for a few weeks?

2 Large or larger?

⏹ Listen to the sentences. Which adjective do you hear? Put a tick next to the word you hear.

1. large ......   larger ......   6. large ......   larger ......
2. high ......   higher ......   7. nice ......   nicer ......
3. big ......   bigger ......   8. safe ......   safer ......
4. wet ......   wetter ......   9. big ......   bigger ......
5. small ......   smaller ......

Compare your answers. Practise saying the two forms of the adjectives.

Listen to some sentences from the same conversation. Write down the sentence in the comparative form.

Example: You hear: *Newcastle is **large**.*
            You write: *Newcastle is **larger**.*

REVIEW OF UNIT 14

1 I haven't broken anything this week   speaking

Have you ever broken anything? Work with a partner and take turns to ask questions and complete this table. Put a tick for everything that your partner has broken.

Example: A: *Have you broken anything big this week?*
           B: *Yes, I have. I broke a vase.*

	Something big	Something small	A bone in your body
This week	......	......	......
This month	......	......	......
This year	......	......	......

Now count up the ticks. Who has broken the most?

2 How did it happen?   the past simple and the present perfect

Study the example.

Example: **I've broken** *one thing this month.* **I was** *in the kitchen, and my daughter* **asked** *me for the milk. I* **turned** *round and* **knocked** *over the tea pot.*

Put the verbs into the right tenses.

1. .... (break) anything this week, Michael?

   Yes, I .... (be) at home in the bathroom and I .... (drop) my watch on the floor. The glass .... (break). So the next day, I .... (buy) a cheap one.

2. Well, I .... never .... (break) an arm, but I .... (break) my leg on a skiing holiday this winter. It .... (be) my first time skiing, and at the end of the first day my teacher .... (say) I .... (be) very good. But when I .... (go) back to the hotel, I .... (fall) down the steps and .... (break) my leg. So that .... (be) the end of my skiing holiday!

In small groups, tell stories about things you've broken this month or this year.

16

OUR NEIGHBOURHOOD

Language focus:
relative pronouns
present perfect with *just* and *yet*
giving directions: imperatives

Vocabulary:
neighbourhoods

A

1 This is my newsagent's, on the corner   speaking

Make a simple drawing or map of your
neighbourhood. Put in all the buildings or
places that are important to you personally.
Show your map to another person and talk
about your two neighbourhoods.

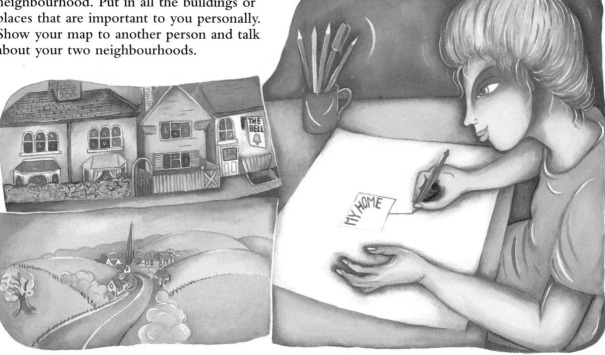

2 There are a lot of markets   vocabulary and speaking

Bring together all the maps that you have drawn. How many of these buildings are
there on your maps?

- ☐ homes of friends
- ☐ churches
- ☐ markets
- ☐ shops
- ☐ banks
- ☐ schools
- ☐ parks
- ☐ cafés
- ☐ homes of family members
- ☐ mosques
- ☐ supermarkets
- ☐ small 'corner' shops
- ☐ petrol stations
- ☐ restaurants
- ☐ bus stops
- ☐ medical centres
- ☐ other buildings or places (name them)

Discuss these questions in groups.

- What do your maps tell people from other countries about your way of life? (Are there lots
  of shops of one kind? Are there lots of restaurants? etc.)
- Are there things in your country that you don't see in other countries? (Are there special
  shops or markets, etc.?)
- Are there interesting similarities or differences in your maps?

3 What does the word neighbourhood mean to you?

reading; relative pronouns

Read the article. Complete the two lists.

Things shown on Ontario maps
petrol stations ....

Things shown on English maps
churches ....

....

....

What does the word neighbourhood mean to you?

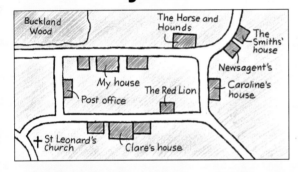

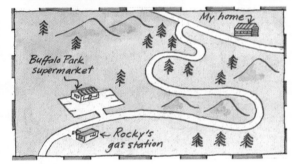

Two scientists who are doing research in psychology at York University have just completed the first part of an interesting study. It shows that people in different countries think in very different ways about their neighbourhoods. The scientists gave a piece of paper to fifty people in Canada and England. They then asked them to draw a map of their neighbourhood. They told people to show on it all the places that were important to them personally.

Of course, the two psychologists can't yet make firm statements about people's attitudes to their neighbourhoods, because they haven't asked enough people. But the maps they've got seem to suggest interesting differences.

For example, in small towns in Ontario, people put on their maps a lot of petrol stations. They also put large supermarkets quite far from their homes. Generally, they did not show many homes of family or friends. Does this show a 'car-culture' society – a society where families live far apart and people drive everywhere?

In England, on the other hand, people drew more churches, more homes of friends or family, more small 'corner' stores – and, of course, the very important 'local', the pub where people get together to chat or play darts.

The two scientists haven't been to other parts of the world yet, but they're planning to start work in Western Australia next. We're waiting for their report on neighbourhood barbecues ...

Are the things on the lists similar to – or different from – the things you put on your map in Exercise 1?

Look at these ways of adding more information about something.

Bring together all the maps **that your groups have drawn**.
Two people **who live in China** have just drawn maps.

Bring together all the maps.
(Which maps? We give more information by adding: **that your groups have drawn**.)
Two people have just drawn maps.
(Which people? We give more information by adding: **who live in China**.)

Use the expressions in the box to give more information about one thing in each sentence.

1. Two scientists have just completed a study.
2. People drew maps of all the places.
3. The study shows a society.
4. An important building in England is the pub.

where families live far apart   that were important to them personally
who are doing research in psychology   where people get together to chat or play darts.

QC Now do the **Quick Check** exercises your teacher will give you.

1 Our neighbours have just moved

⊂⊃ ⊂⊃ Two people are talking about changes in their neighbourhood. Listen and decide which pictures show what has just happened. Number them from 1 to 4.

Think of your street. Has anything just happened there?
Tell the class. Talk about the changes with others.

2 Oh, have you met them yet?

Here are three short conversations. One part is missing. Complete the conversations, using *yet*.

Example: A: *We've got new neighbours.*
   B: ***Have you met them yet?***
   A: *No, not yet. But I'm going over to see them tonight.*

1. A: A new shop has opened right across the street from us.

   B: ....?
   A: Oh, yes, and it's great! It's got all kinds of different things, from all over the world.
2. A: My television set's broken down.

   B: ....?
   A: No, I haven't had time to do that yet.
3. A: My neighbours have had a baby girl!

   B: ....?
   A: Yes, I've been over to the hospital to see her. She's lovely!

Now write a short conversation, with B's part missing. Ask another person to write B's question. Read your conversations to the class.

3 There have been a lot of changes recently | writing a description; discussion |

Choose one of these two writing tasks.

1. Imagine you are writing a paragraph for a local newspaper about changes in your neighbourhood. You can use the following ideas to help you.

Several years ago my neighbourhood was …
It has become much more … Now there are …
I like it much better now because … *or* I don't like it as much now because …

2. Imagine you are writing a letter to friends to tell them about recent changes in your English class. You can use the following ideas to help you if you like.

There have been a few changes in my English class this month.
Some people have …
We've just started …
It has become more … Now we are …
I like it better now because …

QC Now do the **Quick Check** exercises your teacher will give you.

C

1 It's the second street on the right | vocabulary and listening |

Study these expressions. They are used to give directions.

Listen to the recording and choose the right diagram.

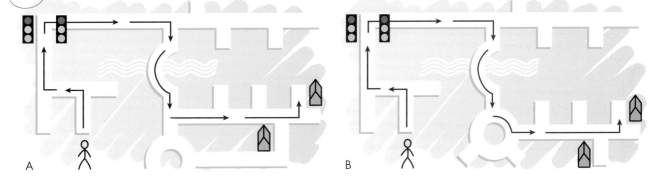

A   B

2 The building is on your right

practice with directions

Work with a partner. Make a map of the neighbourhood around the building where you are learning English. Show a few streets around the building. Put at least two other buildings on your map.

Change partners. Don't show your new partner your map. Give directions to your partner.

Example: A: *Start from our building. Go out of the main entrance. Go straight ahead down Lindas Street. Take the second street on the right. The building is just down the street.*

B: *Is it the bank?*

A: *No, but it's next to the bank.*

B: *Oh, ... is it the shoe shop?*

A: *Yes, it is.*

Can your new partner guess what the building is?

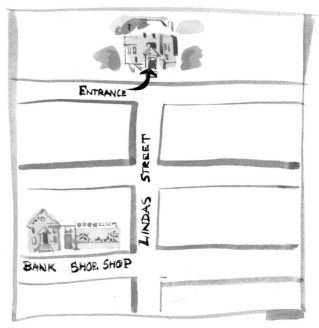

3 From the bus stop, you just cross the road, and you're there

writing directions

Imagine that you've asked people in your class to come to your house. Write a note to give them directions from your English class to your home.

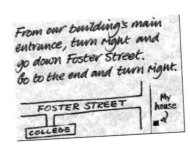

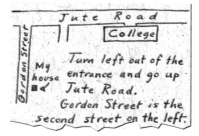

QC Now do the **Quick Check** exercises your teacher will give you.

PERSONAL STUDY WORKBOOK

- present perfect forms
- directions
- reading about neighbourhood sales
- writing an advertisement
- pronunciation work
- visual dictionary – the neighbourhood

REVIEW OF UNIT 14

1 Guess the name of the sport | vocabulary game |

📖 For each sport you will hear five clues. A correct guess after the first clue gets five points, after the second clue four points and so on. One guess only for each clue.

Sport 1 .... Sport 2 .... Sport 3 ....
Sport 4 .... Sport 5 .... Sport 6 ....

2 In my life up to now | present perfect |

Complete the sentences. In what ways have you changed most in your life up to now?

I've become a bit more .... / a lot more ....
I've become a bit less .... / a lot less ....

Think of someone at work or at home. In what ways have they changed in the last few years?

.... has become a bit more .... / a lot more ....
.... has become a bit less .... / a lot less ....

Ask others about the changes they have noted and the reasons for them.

REVIEW OF UNIT 15

1 *Untidy* is the opposite of *tidy* | word-building: prefixes |

Look at these adjectives. Complete the table of opposites.

un	in	im
tidy – **un**tidy	efficient – **in**efficient	polite – **im**polite
important –	expensive –	practical –
exciting –	formal –	patient –
interesting –	convenient –	
friendly –		
safe –		
popular –		
happy –		
crowded –		
polluted –		
usual –		

2 Giving up the piano was a big regret | listening |

📖 Listen to two people talking. Complete the notes.

	Chris	Kate
Biggest regret	*not studying hard enough*	....
Happiest moment	....	....

Listen again and complete the questions. Ask others in the class.

What's the .... regret you've had .... ?
What's been the .... moment in your life .... ?

17

IT'S WORTH DOING WELL

Language focus:	Vocabulary:
adverbs ending in *ly*	how people do things
contrasting adjectives/adverbs	hobbies and crafts
connecting words of sequence	rude/polite actions
imperatives	

A

1 I can do this quickly! | problem solving and discussion; adverbs |

Do two of these puzzles.

A When my father was 32, I was 8. Now he is twice as old as I am. How old am I?

B Can you work out the missing sums?

24

15 17   16

C How many different colour words are hidden in this square?

```
O R Y P N A B G
R D I E Y E L O
A K E B E U E W
N R T R L L C N
G R I P L B I G
E S K B O T E D
L I A N W O R B
D A T E L E I V
```

D Find the things to eat by rearranging the letters in each word.

OOMTETAS

EEESCH

UTTCEEL

Interview others in the class to find out which puzzles they did, and how they did them. Ask these questions. Make a note of the answers.

Which puzzles did you do?
Did you do them quickly (*write Q*) or slowly (*write S*)?

Did people in your class prefer the puzzles with words, or the puzzles with numbers?
Which puzzle did most people do quickly? Which puzzle did most people do slowly?

2 Special skills
listening and discussion; adverbs

Tick the things you can do quickly, easily and confidently in your own language.

1. Add up the cost of your shopping
2. Work out how much thirteen 55 cent stamps cost
3. Divide up a restaurant bill after a meal with a group
4. Give instructions clearly
5. Explain a word to another person who doesn't know it
6. Give a public talk
7. ....
8. ....

Talk about your ticks with another person. Listen to your profile. Is it correct for you?

Choose A, B or C. Do it by yourself or with a partner.

A. Think of two more things to add to the list: one that shows people are good with words, one that shows people are good with numbers.
B. Think of two things that show people are good with their hands: (Example: Can you make a paper airplane or bird?)
C. Think of two things that show people have a good sense of direction: (Example: Can you find your way back to your hotel in a strange city?)

Compare with others who chose a different letter.

3 A good waiter works quickly
adjectives and adverbs contrasted

Complete the sentences to show what you think. Use some of the adverbs in the box. Then compare your ideas with others.

Example: A: *How do you think a good waiter works, Harriet?*
          B: *I think a good waiter works quickly and politely. Do you agree?*

A good dentist works ....
A good politician speaks ....
A good driver drives ....

slowly	quickly	quietly	confidently	patiently	tidily	honestly
noisily	politely	seriously	selfishly	formally	efficiently	carefully

Study these adjectives and adverbs:

slow – slowly   formal – formally   tidy – tidily

Now write the missing adverbs or adjectives.

interesting –	practical –	.... – noisily
nice –	.... – naturally	happy – ....
.... – safely	special –	.... – prettily
sad –	beautiful –	easy – ....
.... – cheaply	.... – usually	.... – busily
expensive –	.... – usefully	untidy – ....

What about the adjective *good*? What is the adverb? ....

Now do the **Quick Check** exercises your teacher will give you.

1 My favourite hobby is ... | vocabulary; speaking |

Match each hobby with a picture. Help each other
with words you don't know – or use a dictionary.
Can you add any hobbies to the list?

> gardening   pottery   photography
> playing a musical instrument
> listening to music   collecting stamps
> origami   painting or drawing
> making jewellery   working with wood
> cooking   walking or hiking   camping

Have you tried these hobbies?
What are your favourite hobbies?

Ask a partner about hobbies they've
tried.

Examples: *Have you ever tried making jewellery?*
           Which hobbies have you tried?

2 Use a small linoleum block | imperatives; adverbs |

Complete these instructions using the words in the box.

Lino printing

With this simple method of
printing, you can make all sorts
of beautiful things, including
writing paper, bags and cards.

1. Use printing ink to print on
   paper.

2. Use a small
   linoleum block.

3. First, ... the shape on the lino block as clearly as you can.

4. Use a special knife. Cut away all the parts around the shape very ....

5. Next, put printing ink onto the lino block.

6. Press the shape .... onto the paper.

7. After that, ... the shape carefully.

8. Repeat this .... to build up a pattern.

> firmly   draw   carefully   remove   regularly

Check your answers. Have you ever tried lino printing? What happened?

3 First you ... [writing]

Write some simple instructions for a craft or hobby. Use a dictionary. Use some of these connecting words.

First, ...

Then, ...

Next, ...

After that, ...

Read your instructions to the class. Can they guess what your hobby is?

QC Now do the **Quick Check** exercises your teacher will give you.

C

1 Is it important to say *please* in your country? [discussion]

How do you say *please* and *thank you* in your language?

Read the four situations below and guess. In English-speaking countries, is it important to say *please*? Is it the same in your country?

	It's important	*It's not important*
– when you ask for the bill in a restaurant	......	......
– when you want something on a table but can't reach it	......	......
– when you ask for a day off at work	......	......
– when you ask someone to move their car	......	......

Read the situations below and guess. In English-speaking countries, is it important to say *thank you*? Is it the same in your country?

	It's important	*It doesn't matter*
– when the waiter brings the meal to your table in a restaurant	......	......
– when someone says you have done something very well	......	......
– when someone opens a door for you in a shop	......	......
– when someone says you look nice	......	......

Compare your ideas in groups.

2 Politeness is one of the most important things listening; writing; discussion

Is it very important to be polite? Listen to three people talking about this. Complete the notes.

	It's important?	Why or why not?
Speaker 1	No	People are sometimes .... Better to say what you mean.
Speaker 2	....	An old English habit – a waste of ....
Speaker 3	....	It shows people that you care about them and about ....

Do you agree with the speakers? Write two sentences to give your opinion.

I agree with Speaker ...... because ....

I don't agree with Speaker ...... because ....

Compare your ideas in groups.

3 Doing things politely – a modern etiquette book reading; rewriting

Read this extract from the beginning of a modern etiquette book. Help each other with any problems.

With a partner, rewrite these sentences so that their meaning matches the text.

Example: *Etiquette is something that happens only at special times.*
Etiquette isn't something that happens only at special times.

1. Being polite is important because it makes life more stressful.
2. Being polite makes the quality of life worse.
3. Politeness really means not thinking about other people.
4. Polite families live unhappy lives.
5. Young people are more formal than older people.
6. It is very hard to learn to be polite.

Check your answers with others. Do you agree with the text?

Chapter 1

ETIQUETTE means acting politely and thoughtfully towards other people. Etiquette is something you think about every day, not only on special occasions. Acting in a polite way improves the quality of life and reduces stress. Families live more happily, business happens more peacefully.

There are no absolute rules for polite behaviour. Customs are different in different parts of the country. Young people are often more relaxed and informal than their parents. But you can't go wrong if you remember that the main rule is to think about other people. Be considerate. And that's a skill you can learn easily.

QC Now do the **Quick Check** exercises your teacher will give you.

PERSONAL STUDY WORKBOOK

- listening to teachers talking about what makes a good learner
- adverbs and adjectives
- vocabulary extension (adverbs and their opposites)
- a reading text about using a video camera
- visual dictionary – hobbies

REVIEW OF UNIT 15

1 Working late is a problem | the -ing sound in sentences; dictation; discussion |

⬭ Listen to these ten sentences. Which ones have an -ing sound in them? Put a tick if there is an -ing sound and a cross if there isn't.

Examples: *I like sitting at my computer.* ☑   *Sit on a good quality chair at work.* ☒

1. ☐   2. ☐   3. ☐   4. ☐   5. ☐   6. ☐   7. ☐   8. ☐   9. ☐   10. ☐

Listen again. Write down the first three sentences. Do you agree with them? Discuss your opinions with a partner.

2 Before leaving the building ... | writing with *before* or *after* + -ing |

Choose three of the sentences. Complete them with an instruction.

Example: *Before leaving the building, please turn off the lights.*

Before leaving the building, ...   Before leaving the hotel, ...   After using this room, ...
Before using the photocopier, ...   After using the computer, ...   After doing this exercise, ...

In small groups, read your sentences. Write similar instructions for your language class.

REVIEW OF UNIT 16

1 I haven't had time yet | writing; discussion |

Write two lists. Then compare your lists in groups.

1. Make a list of things you've started but haven't finished yet.
2. Write down things you intend to do but haven't done yet.

Examples: *List 1: I started a book three weeks ago but I haven't finished it yet.*
          List 2: I'm going to see that new film but I haven't had time yet.

These words may give
you some ideas: letter   gifts   clothes   repairs   photos   to phone   course

2 I like teachers who have lots of ideas | vocabulary; relative pronouns |

Match the two halves of the sentences. Use a relative pronoun to connect them.
Number 1 is an example.

1. I like teachers *who* ....   a. put their toys away.
2. I like restaurants ....   b. are interesting to read.
3. I like shopkeepers ....   c. have lots of ideas.
4. I like children ....   d. the waiters are friendly.
5. I like books ....   e. are very quiet.
6. I like cars ....   f. chat with people.

Divide the class into two.

Learners in Group A: Write part 1 of a sentence like the ones above.
Example: *I like ... (who/where/that)*

Learners in Group B: Write part 2 of a sentence like the ones above.
Example: *... are very noisy.*

Group A: try to find someone in Group B with a good ending to your sentence.

18

ON YOUR TRAVELS

Language focus:
recommendation/advice: *should, shouldn't*
obligation: *has to, have to*
lack of obligation: *doesn't/don't have to*

Vocabulary:
travel, tourism

A

1 Travels and trips   conversation

Write down the number of different countries or places you have travelled to in the past ten years. Let a partner guess the names of the places.

Talk about a recent trip with a partner. Use these questions to help you.

- Where did you go?
- How did you travel? (By plane? By train? By car? By bicycle? On foot?)
- Was your trip fun or boring, enjoyable or terrible? Why?
- Was it a holiday or a business trip?
- What did you enjoy most?
- Was there anything you did not enjoy?
- How long did you stay?

Change partners. How much can you find out about your new partner's trip?

Example: A: *I went to Kenya last year.*
B: *Was it a holiday?*
A: *Yes, I went to see the animals. How about you? Did you go to another country?*

Tell the class one thing you found interesting about your partner's trip.

Example: *Sevdar saw some interesting animals in Kenya.*

2 You should raise your ankles

should/shouldn't; writing lists; discussion

In small groups, write recommendations for air travellers.

> **How to be a good long distance air traveller**
>
> On a long flight …
> – you should take ....
> – you should drink ....
> – you shouldn't drink ....
> – you should ....
> – you shouldn't ....
>
> After arriving in a hot country after a long flight, you should
> ....

Display all the recommendations on the wall of your class, and discuss them. Are there any unusual ideas?

Listen to pairs comparing their recommendations. Complete the table. Put a tick if their ideas are similar to yours and a cross if they are different.

	1 & 2	3 & 4	Similar to your ideas?
On a long flight …			
– you should take	Speaker 1 – loose clothes. Speaker 2 – boiled sweets		....
– you should drink	....	Speaker 3 – water and ….	....
– you shouldn't drink	....		....
– you should	....	Speaker 3 – sleep	....
– you shouldn't	....	....	....
After arriving in a hot country, you should	....	....	....

Do you agree with the advice you've just heard?

3 Visitors to my country

writing

An English-speaking friend is planning to visit your country. Write a short letter to give some advice.

> *Address:* ....
> ....
> *Post code:* ....
> *Date:* ....
>
> *Dear* ....
> It's great to hear that you are planning to visit .... Here are some ideas to help you have a nice time.
>
> *Things to mention:*
> food (You should eat .... You should try ....)
> things to see (You should try to see ....)
> things to bring (You should remember to bring ....)
> things to be careful about (You should be careful about .... You shouldn't stay/buy/travel on ....)
>
> I hope you have a wonderful trip!
> With best wishes,
> *Your name:* ....

QC Now do the **Quick Check** exercises your teacher will give you.

B

1 You have to buy a visa at the airport

have to, should and don't have to; reading

Study the two examples.

Work in groups of three. Each of you reads a different text. Do the True or False exercise on the next page for your text.

obligation

Necessary. Required.
Travellers have to have one.

lack of obligation

Not necessary. It's your choice.
Most travellers don't have to have one.

A

TRAVELLING TO
Kashmir

Visas for India are necessary for travellers from all countries. Travellers have to have two photographs and go to an Indian embassy – not more than six months before the visit. With a visa, travellers can stay for six months in any year. In India, however, no special permission is necessary to visit Kashmir or the Ladakh region.

It is easy to exchange traveller's cheques anywhere in Indian cities. Away from the main cities, however, it can be more difficult, if not impossible. Tourists should take a good supply of the local currency with them.

B

TRAVELLING TO
Turkey

It is not necessary for visitors from most countries to get a visa before going to Turkey. But they have to buy a 90-day tourist visa upon arrival. After 90 days, tourists have to leave the country for a few days at least. They can then re-enter and buy another tourist visa.

Tourists should get some local currency at the airport or entry port. These services are efficient and the exchange rates are good. Some large post offices (but not small ones) accept traveller's cheques. It is a good idea to travel with some cash for emergencies.

C

TRAVELLING TO
Japan

To enter Japan, visas are not required for tourists or business visitors of many nationalities for stays of not more than 90 days. Travellers from some countries, for example Germany, Ireland, Mexico and the U.K. can stay up to six months without a visa. Travellers from some countries, for example Canada, France, Italy, Malaysia, Spain and the U.S.A. can stay up to three months. Visitors from Australia and South Africa cannot enter without a visa. Visas are free, but passport photos and return tickets are required.

Foreign currency or traveller's cheques can be exchanged at 'Authorised Foreign Exchange Banks'. It is usually safe to carry money in the form of cash.

True or False? Write *T* or *F*.

A. Travelling to Kashmir
...... 1. Most travellers don't have to have a visa to enter India.
...... 2. Travellers have to go to an Indian embassy to get a visa.
...... 3. Tourists don't have to have any photos for their visa.
...... 4. Travellers with Indian visas don't have to have special permission to visit Kashmir.
...... 5. It's not a good idea to take any local currency.

B. Travelling to Turkey
...... 1. Visitors from most countries have to get a visa before travelling to Turkey.
...... 2. When you arrive in Turkey, you have to buy a visa.
...... 3. Tourists with a visa have to leave after 30 days.
...... 4. It's a good idea to get local currency when you arrive.
...... 5. It isn't a good idea to travel with cash for emergencies.

C. Travelling to Japan
...... 1. Tourists from many countries don't have to have a visa for the first 90 days of their stay.
...... 2. English tourists don't have to have a visa for the first year.
...... 3. Americans don't have to have a visa for the first 3 months.
...... 4. Australians have to have photos and a return ticket to get a visa for Japan.
...... 5. It isn't a good idea to carry cash.

Tell the others in your group about travelling to the country you read about. Have any of these conditions changed, do you think?

2 You don't have to have a passport | have to / don't have to; speaking |

What do people from other countries have to do before visiting your country? Complete the sentences to tell a partner what you know.

People from .... have to ....
People from .... don't have to ....
All visitors have to ....

Are things changing? Is it getting easier to go from one country to another?

3 Travellers should take a hat | obligation, lack of obligation and recommendation; writing sentences |

What do these sentences mean?

It's a good idea. (Mark them G.)
It's required, an obligation. (Mark them R.)
It's not required. (Mark them NR.)

...... 1. Travellers to hot countries should take a hat.
...... 2. Passengers have to check in on time.
...... 3. On business trips, you should take business cards.
...... 4. Tourists should carry traveller's cheques.
...... 5. You don't have to pay airport departure tax.
...... 6. Australians have to get visas to travel to Japan.
...... 7. The Dutch don't have to have a passport to go to France.
...... 8. Travellers in hotels should be quiet at night.
...... 9. You have to have two photos for passports.
...... 10. Air travellers should drink lots of water.

With a partner, write three other sentences. Read your sentences to others. Ask them to say what kind of sentences they are: G, R or NR.

QC Now do the **Quick Check** exercises your teacher will give you.

C

1 What is a good tourist? [reading; writing; discussion]

Read these sentences. With a partner rewrite the sentences you don't agree with.

A good tourist is someone who doesn't eat the local food.
A good tourist is someone who doesn't go to quiet places because it encourages tourism.
A good tourist is someone who spends a lot of money on souvenirs.
A good tourist is someone who tries to use a few words of the local language.
A good tourist is someone who collects bits of rock and flowers.
A bad tourist is someone who takes a lot of photos of local people working.
A bad tourist is someone who respects the history and culture of the country they're visiting.
A bad tourist is someone who sits in the sun and doesn't go anywhere.

Which sentences are the most important? Discuss them with other learners.

2 A good tourist is somebody who respects the traditions [listening; speaking]

⬜⬜ ⬜⬜ Listen to four people talking about tourists. Make notes under the two headings.

Good tourists   *Bad tourists*

Do you agree with the opinions you've heard? Do you have any stories to tell about tourists, like Speaker 3? Tell them to the class.

3 Is tourism good for countries? [listening and discussion; writing]

⬜⬜ Listen to three people talking about tourism. Complete what they say.

Speaker 1:
Tourism is .... for my country. Because I come from .... and it is an island. So it's good for us to have people from other countries coming in.

Speaker 2:
I think tourism is good because people from different countries .... each other, and talk and .... a little bit about each other's country. But sometimes .... people means you don't really know what the country's like, because it's full of ....

Speaker 3:
I think tourism is .... countries because it provides the country with .... money. But it can also spoil the character, sometimes of small villages.

What do you think about tourism? Think of examples from your country if you can. Share your ideas with others. Then write a paragraph about tourism. Give your opinions and your reasons.

QC Now do the **Quick Check** exercises your teacher will give you.

PERSONAL STUDY WORKBOOK

- *should* and *have to*
- *go to ...* and *go to **the** ...*
- pronunciation of /f/ and /v/
- reading on travel and health
- listening and form filling
- visual dictionary – travelling

REVIEW OF UNIT 16

1 I've bought something that's orange | revision of *just* with present perfect |

Think of a thing you have just bought or imagine one. Complete these sentences.

I've just bought something that's .... (colour)
I've just bought something that's about the same size as ....
I've just bought something that's made of .... (metal, plastic, wool, leather, etc.)
I've just bought something that's useful for ....

Say your sentences to a partner. Can your partner guess what it is?

REVIEW OF UNIT 17

1 Read these carefully | adverbs and instructions |

Read these instructions. What are they for? Choose adverbs to put in the green spaces.

tightly   carefully

1. Place your paper onto the glass .... Choose the copy size, and number of copies. Insert the coin, or coins. Press the green copy button. Remove your paper from the glass. Press the 'Clear' button.

   These are instructions for making a ....

2. Place the hand in cool water immediately. Cover it with a clean bandage. Be careful not to tie the bandage too ....

   These are instructions for treating someone with a ....

2 We have reprimanded him severely | listening for adverbs |

Read this letter quickly.

Trading Post Stores
Grenfell Plaza, Edmonton

12th July

Dear Mr Johns,

Thank you for your letter. We are always very happy to get letters from our customers. However, we were sorry to hear about your unhappy experience with our shop assistant. He behaved very badly. I can only say that this is not what we teach the staff in our company, and we have reprimanded him.

We are enclosing a free voucher. Please use it when you are next in one of our shops.

Yours,

J. Bean

J. Bean
Customer Services Manager
Trading Post Stores

⟐ Listen to the manager's letter on the dictaphone. It is different from the one in the book. Change two words that are wrong, and add three missing adverbs.

19

A LOOK AT LIFE!

Language focus:	Vocabulary:
expressing wishes with *would like*: positive, negative, question forms	views on life how people spend time
would with other verbs	beauty

A

1 Life is just a bowl of cherries [speaking]

Read these sayings about life:

Life is just a bowl of cherries.
Life is sweet.
Life is what you make it.

Life is hard, nasty and short.
A life lived in fear is only half a life.

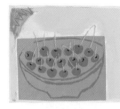

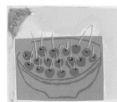

Do you have any sayings about life in your language? Think of a saying you like and tell a partner why. You can choose one of the sayings above if you prefer.

2 Is your life in balance? [vocabulary; speaking]

Think about your life at
the moment. Put expressions
from the box into the
appropriate scales.

I have enough. *It's about right.* *I have too much.* *I don't have enough.*

exercise	sleep	work	free time	time for myself	time with friends

exercise   sleep   work   free time   time for myself   time with friends
time to read   time to think   time to relax   time with my family
time with ....   time to help others   time to travel   time to ....

Compare your scales with a partner. Ask and answer questions about the things you've
written in the *I don't have enough* or *I have too much* scale.

Example: A: *Would you like more time to relax?*
B: *No, I wouldn't.*
A: *Why not?*
B: *Life's too short. What about you? I see you'd like more time with your family.*
A: *Yes, I would. I'd like to see my children more.*

3 What would grandparents like? [writing]

What do you think these people would like?

1. A busy parent:
   I think she'd like .... because ....

2. A teenager:
   I think he'd like .... because ....

3. Grandparents:
   I think they'd like .... because ....

4. A close friend of yours:
   I think .... because ....

In groups, read your sentences to each other
and talk about them.

*I'd like to see my
grandchildren more.*

4 I'd like to have a long holiday [listening]

⚏ Listen to two people talking about what they would like. Make notes on what they
say. What does each one do?

Speaker 1 is a ....
Speaker 2 is a ....

Check your answers with others.

QC Now do the **Quick Check** exercises your teacher will give you.

1 I'd like to live in a world that's clean   writing; reading aloud

Complete the sentence using between one and five words. In a group, put your sentences together to build a poem.

I'd like to live in a world that's ....

When you are ready, read the poem aloud to the class.

2 A world that's kind to children   listening

Two groups have built poems with their sentences. Listen to them.

3 Would you like to live to be 100 years old?   would ('d) with other verbs; writing

Work in a group of three. Talk about this question:

Would you like to live to be 100 years old?

Together, make a list of the advantages and disadvantages of a very long life.

Advantages (+)

....

....

....

Disadvantages (-)

....

....

....

Study these examples:

I'd like to live to be 100 years old. **On the one hand**, it would be fun to see the new machines of the future, and to be a great grandparent. **On the other hand**, I would get tired all the time, and I wouldn't enjoy that very much.

I wouldn't like to live to be 100 years old, because I'd probably be sick all the time. I would keep forgetting things. It wouldn't be very nice. **On the other hand**, I'd know a lot after a hundred years. And perhaps someone would listen to me.

Now write a paragraph starting:

I'd like to live to be 100 years old …
or
I wouldn't like to live to be 100 years old …

Use your table of advantages and disadvantages.

QC Now do the **Quick Check** exercises your teacher will give you.

1 A question of beauty   `discussion`

Look at these faces. Which one do you think is the most beautiful? Compare your ideas with others and try to give reasons.

2 The perfect look?   `reading; discussion`

Study this title from a newspaper article:

CREATING THE WORLD'S PERFECT LOOK ON COMPUTER

Guess: What is it about? Read the text quickly without a dictionary.

WHEN PEOPLE say, *She's got a beautiful face*, what exactly do they like about it? Traditionally, people thought that beauty was an individual thing, but this is not true. Psychologists at New Mexico State University have developed a computer technique that draws a 'beautiful' face from the choices made by men and women.

Psychologists showed 30 computer images of women's faces to 40 students (men and women). They asked the students to give each picture a score from 1 (not beautiful at all) to 10 (perfect). The computer then used the pictures with high scores to draw new images until finally one of the pictures got a perfect 10. The computer then combined the 40 faces with the highest scores to produce the most beautiful face of all, out of 17 billion possible computer images.

After studying the most beautiful face, the scientists discovered that it is similar to the face of ....

Shut the book and write down two things you remember from the text. Read them to a partner. Have you both remembered similar things?

Read the text again carefully. Write something in the space at the end of the text. Talk about your guess with a partner.

3 So what did they discover? `listening; discussion`

▭▭ ▭▭ Listen to two people discussing their guesses. What do they think?

The woman thinks the most beautiful face is a ....

The man thinks the most beautiful face is similar to the face of ....

Now listen to someone reading the missing part of the text. Complete this sentence.

Scientists discovered that the most beautiful face is similar to the face of ....

Look again at the face you chose in Exercise 1. Is it similar to the face that the computer created? What do you think of the article? Talk about your views.

QC Now do the **Quick Check** exercises your teacher will give you.

PERSONAL STUDY WORKBOOK

- form and uses of *would*
- writing a paragraph
- visual dictionary – what we would like to do and be

D ▬ REVIEW AND DEVELOPMENT

REVIEW OF UNIT 17

1 I speak more quickly than my brother `adverbs; comparative forms of adverbs`

Write in the missing adverb forms. Check your answers with a partner.

quick – quickly   good – ....
clear – clearly   polite – politely
easy – ....   careful – ....
gentle – ....   peaceful – ....

Use some of the words to compare yourself to friends or others in your family.

I can .... more quickly than ....
I .... more easily than ....
I play .... (a sport or an instrument) well, but my .... plays much
  better than I do.
I .... more .... than ....

Talk about your sentences with others.

Example: *I drive more carefully than my brother. He's a terrible driver; he's had lots of accidents.*

2 Adverb mime `revision of adverbs`

Work in pairs. Choose an adverb. Don't tell the other pairs. Ask one person from another pair to mime the adverb. Try to guess the adverb.

Example: One pair chooses the adverb *slowly*.
          Another pair says: *Eat your breakfast* **like this**, *Pedro.*
          One of the first pair mimes eating breakfast *slowly*.
          The others try to guess the adverb.
          If the guess is not correct they give another instruction: *Walk* **like this**, *Pedro.*

REVIEW OF UNIT 18

1 The shoe shops were shut | pronunciation /ʃ/ and question intonations |

Read the conversation, and underline the parts of the words that have the sound /ʃ/ as in *shop*.

Did you have a good weekend, Sheila?	No, terrible … shocking.
Why was that?	I planned to go walking.
Don't you like walking?	Yes, but I hadn't got any good shoes.
Couldn't you buy shoes?	Yes, I got some cash and went shopping. But the shoe shops were shut.
So what did you do?	I packed my old shoes.
That's all right then.	Well … I had a reservation for the 4 o'clock train.
So what did you do?	I asked permission to leave work early.
What did your boss say?	He said short days are not efficient.
What happened then?	We got into a long discussion.
Oh dear. And what then?	I got to the station late.
Did you miss the train?	Yes, I just missed it.
So what did you do?	I cried and went home.

🎧 Listen and check your answers.

Listen to the conversation again. This time, you ask Sheila the questions.

2 I got a cheap charter flight | pronunciation /tʃ/ and question intonation |

Read the conversation, and underline the parts of the words that have the sound /tʃ/ as in *check*.

Charles, hello!	
Did you have a good trip?	It was great!
Where did you go?	I got a cheap charter to Chicago.
Did you get to the airport on time?	Yes, I had time to check in, and change some traveller's cheques.
Did you have a good flight?	Wonderful. The flight attendants were cheerful. There was a great choice for lunch – chicken or cheese omelette, and some delicious chocolates.
Did you have a good book?	No, but I had a nice chat with the person next to me – charming man.
Was there a good film?	I watched a film about children. It gave me a headache.
So what did you do?	I fell asleep.

🎧 Listen and check your answers.

Listen to the conversation again. This time, you ask Charles the questions.

3 I lost all my cheques! | pronunciation /ʃ/ and /tʃ/ |

🎧 Listen to some travellers saying what they lost. After each sentence, show the sound that you hear.

If you hear the sound /ʃ/ as in **sh**op: raise one hand.

If you hear the sound /tʃ/ as in **ch**eck: raise two hands.

20

I'M SO SORRY!

Language focus:	Vocabulary:
apologising	shops and shopping situations
complaining	hotel situations

A

1 I bought my watch at the duty-free shop — conversation

Choose one thing that you have with you today. Tell the person next to you where you bought it and talk about it.

Example: A: *Where did you buy it?*
B: *I bought/got it at the duty-free shop.*
A: *How many years have you had it?*
B: *I've had it for about five years.*
A: *Do you like it? Have you ever had any problems with it?*

2 You can pay with a credit card — vocabulary and speaking

Complete the flow chart. Put the expressions below into the appropriate boxes.

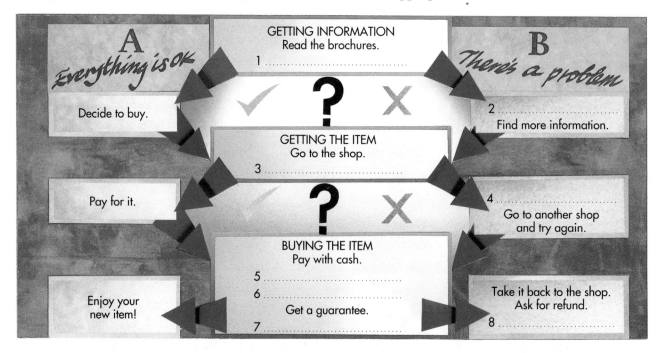

A Everything is OK

GETTING INFORMATION
Read the brochures.
1 ....

B There's a problem

Decide to buy.

2 ....
Find more information.

GETTING THE ITEM
Go to the shop.
3 ....

Pay for it.

4 ....
Go to another shop and try again.

BUYING THE ITEM
Pay with cash.
5 ....
6 ....
Get a guarantee.

Enjoy your new item!
7 ....

Take it back to the shop. Ask for refund.
8 ....

Get a receipt.   Pay with a credit card.   Ask to see another item.   Decide not to buy.
Ask for the item.   Pay by cheque.   Ask the shop for information.   Decide not to buy.

Answer these questions and talk about them with others.

- In your country is it easy to get information before you buy something?
- Can you usually pay by cheque or credit card?
- Do you always get a guarantee? Is it important to get a receipt?
- There's a problem. Can you usually get a refund easily? Can you exchange things easily?

3 Can I try it on, please?   vocabulary; writing a dialogue

Here are two shopping conversations. Write an appropriate reply for the shop assistant. You can choose some of the sentences in the box.

1.

CUSTOMER:	Can I try it on, please?
SHOP ASSISTANT:	....
CUSTOMER:	Have you got a bigger size?
SHOP ASSISTANT:	....
CUSTOMER:	Is there a cheaper one?
SHOP ASSISTANT:	....
CUSTOMER:	I'd like a different colour.
SHOP ASSISTANT:	....

Oh, but the blue looks so nice on you!
Yes, madam, please come this way.
Yes, we've got a size 20.
I'm afraid that's the only colour we've got.
Well, there is, but it's not the same quality, of course.

2.

CUSTOMER:	Excuse me. I bought this last week and now it's stopped. I don't think it's very good quality.
SHOP ASSISTANT:	....
CUSTOMER:	But it's not working, so I'd like a refund.
SHOP ASSISTANT:	....
CUSTOMER:	Here's the receipt.
SHOP ASSISTANT:	....
CUSTOMER:	I want a refund, not the manager.
SHOP ASSISTANT:	....

I'm so sorry about that. Can I see your receipt?
Thank you, sir. If you can just wait a moment, the manager can see you.
I'm sorry, sir, but I have to get the manager. She's the only one who can give refunds.
Have you got your receipt with you?
I'm sorry. That's rather unusual. They're usually very reliable.

With a partner, read out your conversations.

4 I'm terribly sorry   listening and speaking

Imagine that someone buys a new watch and it goes wrong. They take it back to the shop. Here are some examples of what a shop assistant in an English-speaking country can say. What do you think: Which are polite? Are any of them rude?

1. I'm terribly sorry, madam. I have to get the manager. Would you mind waiting here for a moment?
2. I'm sorry about that. Can I see your receipt, please?
3. Wait a moment. I have to find the manager.
4. Can I see your receipt?
5. I'm sorry. That's very unusual. That watch is usually very reliable. Can I have a look at it, please?
6. When did you buy it? Have you got your receipt?

▢▢ Listen to two shop assistants replying to a customer. Tick the sentence each one uses.

Which shop assistant was more polite? Is the attitude of the customer important?

Talk in groups about a time when you took something back to a shop or store. Where were you? What happened? What did you say? What did the shop manager say? Some people say shop assistants are becoming less polite. Do you agree? Does it matter?

QC Now do the **Quick Check** exercises your teacher will give you.

B

1 My room's too cold   vocabulary

Read these complaints. With a partner, match each problem with one or more of the shops and places in the box.

Example: *This ring is too small for my finger.* **jewellers**

1. This doesn't fit.
2. There's a button missing.
3. The lights don't work.
4. The soup is cold.
5. The room's too cold.

6. The air conditioning doesn't work.
7. This is the worst service I've ever had on any flight.
8. Look at this necklace I bought – the diamonds are not real.
9. The cookery course wasn't long enough.

    hotel   fashion shop   college   garage   restaurant   plane   jewellers

2 This cappuccino's cold!   writing and guessing

Look at these shops. Imagine you have a problem in two of them. Write down one sentence to say about each problem.

    café   health food shop   chemists   bookshop   video shop   jewellers
    department store   duty-free shop

Say your sentences to others. Can they guess the shop?

Example: *This cappuccino's cold. Can I have another one, please?* **café**

3 I never complain   listening and discussion

Do you complain when things are not right – in shops, hotels, restaurants? Put a cross (X) on the line to show your opinion.

In shops:
I never complain. _____ I complain a lot.
In hotels or restaurants:
I never complain. _____ I complain a lot.

Compare your crosses with others and talk about any differences between you.

▯▯ ▯▯ Listen to two people talking about when they complain. Answer the questions.

Conversation 1:
Does the man complain a lot? Why or why not? Does he get angry, or does he stay polite?

Conversation 2:
Does the woman complain when she's in other countries? Why or why not? Does she complain in her own country?

Check your answers with a partner.

4 Is there a problem with the light?   mime

Imagine that you are in a hotel in a foreign country. You don't speak the language. Your teacher is going to tell you a problem. Mime your problem to the hotel receptionists (the class). Can they guess the problem?

QC Now do the **Quick Check** exercises your teacher will give you.

C

1 Cultural confusions `discussion; reading`

Work in groups. Choose one of these questions to discuss.

1. Can you think of a situation where people from another country behaved in a way that seemed unusual in your country?
2. Can you think of a situation where something that is usual in your culture seemed unusual in another culture?

Exchange ideas with people who chose the other question.

Work in groups of three. Each person: read a different story.

a

AN AMERICAN BUSINESSMAN was on his way back to America today a week earlier than planned – and he was definitely not very happy about it. Mr Gus Ferry is the head of a middle-sized computer firm in the United States. He went to Japan for the first time to meet the Managing Director of a Japanese computer firm. The morning of their meeting was very hot, and Mr Ferry arrived in shorts. The Japanese Managing Director reacted angrily. He decided not to sign the contract, and Mr Ferry went home again the next day. 'I just don't understand,' he said to reporters at the airport. 'In California, I wear shorts all the time!'

b

I think I told you that Bözkurt invited me to a big party at their home the other day. My friends at the office told me to take flowers, so I bought a big bouquet of roses. That was fine. The food was absolutely wonderful, especially the kebabs, and everyone was friendly to me. People asked me a lot of questions about my work and family. But then about half way through the evening I noticed something terrible. Everybody else in the room had socks or little slippers on, not shoes. Nobody had shoes on at all, except me! I just felt terrible about it ... I didn't know what to say!

c

TIPS FOR VISITORS

Be careful when you say sorry!

A VIETNAMESE WOMAN visiting an American city had a road accident recently, when a motorhome hit the back of her car. No one was hurt. She got out of the car. A policeman and some other people came to look at the accident. She was confused and said to them in English, 'I'm sorry, very sorry'. It was normal for her to say that, but it wasn't the right thing to say in that situation. Because she said she was sorry, the insurance company said the accident was her fault. She had to pay for the repairs!

Tell the other two the story you read. What was the cultural problem in your story?

Together, discuss the stories. Which one do you think was the biggest problem?

2 Mr and Mrs Smith regret | reading; apologies |

Read these different apologies.

1. Mr and Mrs Smith regret that they are unable to attend the wedding of Jane Phillips and John Jones on February 28th at …

2. 'We're sorry we can't come, but Jim's back is bad and he can't move …'

3. We regret that from time to time your choice of meal may not be available owing to previous customer selection.

4. 'AN apologises to passengers for the cancellation of the 15.30 service to Perth. We regret any inconvenience caused.'

5. 'I'm ever so sorry, I just completely forgot about the time. Please don't be too annoyed, darling.'

6. 'I didn't mean to knock it over, it was a complete accident. I just never saw it and then when it broke, it was too late.'

7. 'Sorry, mate, my fault. Let me buy you another. Two more coffees, please.'

8. 'I'm sorry to put you to all this trouble, but Jim's car's at the garage and I've got to get to the airport to meet my mother.'

9. Lewis and Co apologises for the poor quality of the product purchased by you. The company is pleased to offer you a replacement or a full refund, whichever is preferred, and trusts that you will continue to offer your custom at our stores.

Match each apology with the appropriate situation.

a. two people in a café
b. asking a friend for their car
c. an airline menu card
d. a letter from a store
e. someone is late for a date
f. an accident in someone's house
g. a travel announcement
h. a written reply to an invitation
i. a spoken reply to an invitation

Which texts use formal language and which use informal language?

Do you apologise in the same way in your culture in the same situations?

3 I'm sorry, I completely forgot | writing short notes of apology |

Write a short note of apology to one of these people:

– An English friend (You arranged to meet in town but you forgot all about it.)
– Your English teacher (You have to leave the course early because you are going to another country.)
– A friend from New Zealand (She wants to visit you but you have already arranged for other visitors to come at the same time.)
– (Imagine another situation.)

QC Now do the **Quick Check** exercises your teacher will give you.

PERSONAL STUDY WORKBOOK

- pronunciation work
- language for apologies and complaints
- listening to a story about a complaint
- reading and writing about different kinds of apology
- visual dictionary – types of shop

REVIEW OF UNIT 18

1   You shouldn't swim in the rivers | reading and vocabulary |

Which sentences are true for your country? Tick them.

In my country ...
– you have to pay for every visit to the doctor.
– you have to pay for every visit to the dentist.
– you don't have to have health insurance.
– you don't have to pay for emergency treatment in hospital.
– you shouldn't drink water from the tap.
– you shouldn't swim in the rivers; they are polluted.
– you should be careful of insects (mosquitoes, for example).
– you shouldn't try to phone a doctor at night, because they don't usually come to your home at night. You should always go to a hospital.

Check your answers with others – or, if you come from different countries, compare them.

2   You have to work hard | writing |

Work in small groups. Choose one of these topics:

Learning English   Driving in a crowded city   Looking after a small child
Going skiing (or some other activity) for the first time   Choosing a husband or wife
Buying a new house or flat

Complete four sentences about your topic.

You have to ....
You don't have to ....
You should ....
You shouldn't ....

Join another group. Read your sentences to each other. Do you agree with the other group's sentences?

REVIEW OF UNIT 19

1   I wouldn't like to be an actor | writing with *wouldn't like*; reading |

Complete each sentence. You can use one of the words and expressions in the box. Write the sentences on a piece of paper.

I wouldn't like to be ...   The teacher wouldn't like to be ...
I wouldn't like to go to ...   The teacher wouldn't like to go to ...
I wouldn't like to have ...   The teacher wouldn't like to have ...

an actor   a fax machine   a dog   the seaside   a teenager   Antarctica
British   fit   rich   a teacher   a psychiatrist   the bottom of the sea
a computer   a night-time job   a part-time job   perfect   a spider
nights without sleep   a toothache   a baby

Put all your pieces of paper in a box. Pick one out and read the sentences to the class. Guess who wrote them.

21

ALL YOU NEED IS LOVE ... OR MONEY

Language focus:	Vocabulary:
need/want + noun or infinitive	money, needs, success in life
don't need / *don't want* + noun or infinitive	

A

1 A good start in life   need + noun; need + to; speaking and writing

Imagine you have a child or young friend of about seventeen. You can give them *one* gift to help them get a good start in life. Choose the thing that you think is the most important as your gift.

an average salary for a year   a finance and management course
a course on being a good parent
a course on how to respect yourself and love others   a round-the-world air ticket
a few words of advice   a year working on a farm or in a factory

Write a note to the young person.
Explain why your gift is so important.

Read your note to others.
What was the most popular gift in your class? Was money more important than other things?

> Dear ....,
> We need many things in life, but we can't have them all. I'm giving you .... because I think a young person needs to ....

2 Money can't buy you love ⬚ discussion

Look at these sayings about money. Match the sayings with the meanings.

1. Money makes the world go round.
2. Money can't buy you love.
3. The love of money is the root of all evil.
4. Money doesn't grow on trees.

a. Money is the worst thing in the world if you value it too highly.
b. You really need money, it's the most important thing in the world.
c. You have to work to get money.
d. You don't need money, but you do need love.

Which of the three ideas is closest to what you think?
Do you know any sayings in your language about money?

3 I don't need much money ⬚ need / don't need + noun or infinitive; discussion; listening

What is your attitude to money? Has it changed since you were younger? Tick the
statements you agree with now, or agreed with when you were younger. Add one
other statement.

	Younger	*Now*
I don't need more money (I've got enough).	......	......
I always need more money (I never seem to have enough).	......	......
I want to save money for the future.	......	......
I don't need to save money.	......	......
I worry a lot about money.	......	......
I never worry about money.	......	......
Other:	......	......

Compare your opinions with others in the class.

4 I think about money all the time ⬚ listening

⬚⬚ ⬚⬚ Listen to Jim, Jane and Mike talking about money. Match the beginnings of
the sentences with the right endings.

1. Jim thinks about money all the time because
2. Jane worries about money because
3. Mike worries about money because
4. Mike's wife tells him not to worry because
5. When Jane saves up a bit
6. Jane's parents never saved because
7. Mike's parents told him to be careful with
   money because

a. they've always had enough money.
b. it doesn't grow on trees.
c. she's bought a flat.
d. it all goes very quickly.
e. they never had much money.
f. he hasn't got any.
g. he's got two children and a big car.

Check your answers. Are the speakers'
attitudes similar to yours?

⬚⬚ Now do the **Quick Check** exercises your teacher will give you.

1 A stock exchange is a busy place   [vocabulary; discussion]

What is your reaction to these places?

Which of the expressions in the box
do you associate with stockbrokers
(people who work in these places)?

> rich   very busy   very stressed   happy
> able to relax at home after their busy day

Compare your ideas with others.
Would you like to be a stockbroker?

Tokyo
Stock Exchange

New York
Stock Exchange

2 We are what we earn   [reading; discussion]

Match the expressions in Column A with their meanings in Column B.

Column A (expressions)	Column B (meanings)
greatest fear	the money people get for their work
strongest anxiety	useful for the community
is secure financially	what a person is most afraid of
a salary	to receive money for work
valuable to society	what a person is most worried about
to earn	has enough money

Check your answers with others.

Read this text about a stockbroker. Help each other with difficulties.

I WANT TO tell you about Bob Hainemann. He works at the New York Stock Exchange; he always dresses in a grey suit, and he always worries about money. He admits that he has a lot of good things in his life: he married a nice woman named Lois; they have a nice little daughter; they live in a nice little suburb. But he is worried because he is not as secure financially as his parents were. His greatest fear is of *never having enough*. He always wants more. As he tells me about that, I realise that Bob is always going to worry, because the fear of *never having enough* is one of the strongest anxieties in American life.

Money, of course, says a lot about us, and about our place in society. We always want higher salaries. With a high salary, we think, we are better people, more valuable to society. We can say that money isn't important to us, but our attitude towards money tells us a lot about ourselves and about our society. And in our society, we are what we earn.

Make a list of details about Bob, under these headings:

Good things in his life   *Bad things in his life*

Five people wrote down an idea from paragraph 2 that they found interesting. Read what they wrote.

People with high salaries receive more respect in society.
Money is the most important thing in anybody's life.
Our attitude to money shows the kind of person we are.
People say that money isn't important, but it is.
Our salary is our life.

Do you agree with any of these statements? Are there any ideas that you find interesting in paragraph 2? Compare your ideas with others.

3 A letter to the editor | writing a short letter |

Write a very short letter to the magazine to show your opinion of the article about Bob and money.

Read your letters in groups and discuss them.

Dear Madam/Sir,
I read your article about money in a recent issue of your magazine. I think that ...

QC Now do the **Quick Check** exercises your teacher will give you.

C

1 I don't need to go to university | listening |

Listen to three people talking about their needs and wants and complete the summary.

1. Janina .... to study Spanish but she .... really .... it for her job. She .... to go on a holiday in Mexico.
2. Olga .... a child but she ....'t .... to give up her job and she .... the money.
3. Jim d............... .... to go to university because he's 75 years old but he .... to be a student again and he certainly .... to sit at home in front of the TV for the rest of his life.

2 You don't need to do that | grammar practice; discussion |

Study these examples:

A: *I want a new pen but I don't want to spend any money and I don't really need one – my old pen still works.*
B: *I've got a new pen and I never use it. Here you are, you can have it.*
A: *You don't need to do that.*
B: *I know I don't need to, but I want to.*

Choose three of these and make complete sentences to show the things you want, or need.

I need ...   I don't need ...   I want ...   I don't want ...
I need to ...   I don't need to ...   I want to ...   I don't want to ...

Talk to a partner about your sentences.

3 To be a success, you need ... | writing; reading; discussion |

Complete this sentence.

To be a success, you need to ...

Read out your sentences to the class. Make a list of all the things mentioned.

Seven people completed the sentence for a magazine survey. Read their answers.

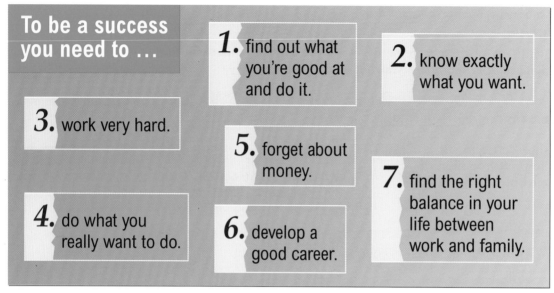

To be a success you need to ...

1. find out what you're good at and do it.

2. know exactly what you want.

3. work very hard.

5. forget about money.

7. find the right balance in your life between work and family.

4. do what you really want to do.

6. develop a good career.

Choose two sentences that seem interesting to you. Tell a partner why you agree or disagree.

QC Now do the **Quick Check** exercises your teacher will give you.

PERSONAL STUDY WORKBOOK

- vocabulary exercises on collocation
- prepositions after *need/want*
- a reading text about choosing the right job
- listening about what you need to be happy
- visual dictionary – money

D   REVIEW AND DEVELOPMENT

REVIEW OF UNIT 19

1 Key or keep? | pronunciation: final consonants |

Listen to six sentences. Do you hear a or b?

1. a. It's your key.
2. a. I like a bed every night.
3. a. I liked it when we were at the shop.
4. a. That's not to say I'm scared.
5. a. I'd like a credit card.
6. a. He likes meat.

b. It's yours to keep.
b. I lie in bed every night.
b. I like it when we work at the shop.
b. That's not too safe. I'm scared.
b. I like a credit card.
b. He likes me.

Say one sentence from each line quickly. Your partner guesses which one it is.

2 Some of my friends are psychologists | pronunciation of consonant clusters |

Study these examples:

Some of my friends are psychologists.
Some of my friends are psychologists and dentists.
Some of my friends are psychologists, dentists and artists.

How many jobs ending with the letters 'sts' can you add to the list? Take turns to say the list. Can you add four more jobs to the list?

🎧 Listen to this list. Which job in the list doesn't end in 'sts'?

REVIEW OF UNIT 20

1 I'm sorry, it was an accident | vocabulary: nouns; adjectives |

Write the adjectives that go with the nouns. (Use a dictionary.)

Noun	Adjective	Noun	Adjective
possibility	....	accident	....
confidence	....	danger	....
tidiness	....	stupidity	....
patience	....	importance	....

Now use each one of the adjectives in a sentence.

1. A: Watch out! You've knocked over the vase!
   B: I'm sorry, that was totally .... !
2. A: Your daughter ran in front of my car!
   B: I'm very sorry. I'm sure she didn't realise it was ....
3. A: Your children have made a mess of this room!
   B: Oh dear, I'm sorry. They've never been very ...., I'm afraid.
4. A: Slow down! I can't type as fast as that!
   B: I'm so sorry. I should be more ....
5. A: Now look what you've done! You've put all my letters into the wrong files!
   B: Sorry. I guess that was rather ....
6. A: Oh, you've got a letter from *Travel Magazine*. What does it say?
   B: It says: The editor regrets that it wasn't .... to include your article in the January magazine.
7. A: You didn't tell me you couldn't come.
   B: Oh, I'm terribly sorry. I just didn't think it was very ....
8. A Look, I'm sure you'll be all right at the interview. Just don't show that you're nervous.
   B: Well, I'm sorry, but I can't. I'm not very ....

🎧 Now listen to the recording and check your answers. In pairs read out the dialogues.

2 Oh dear, I'm sorry | apologies |

🎧 Now listen to some complaints and reply with a short apology.

Example: *Watch out! You've knocked over the vase!*
        (Give an apology) *I'm very sorry.*

22

THE RIGHT CLIMATE?

Language focus:
what's it like questions
if clauses + imperatives or present simple
when clauses + imperatives or present simple

Vocabulary:
weather, climate,
protection against the weather

A

1 Average temperatures in January   discussion; guessing; listening

What is the average temperature for January in your town or city? Do you know? Do other people in the class know?

Look at these average temperatures for January in different cities. Guess the missing temperatures. Compare with a partner.

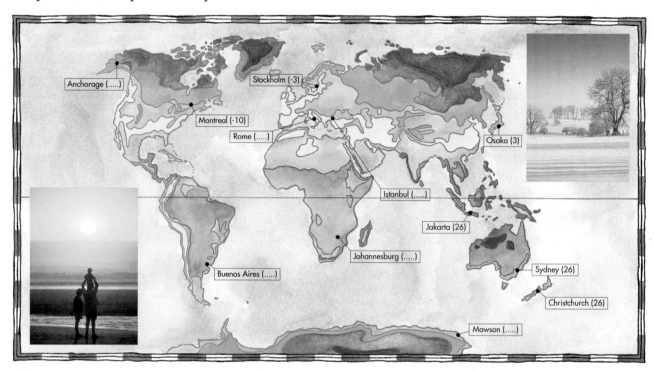

Anchorage (.....)
Stockholm (-3)
Montreal (-10)
Rome (.....)
Osaka (3)
Istanbul (.....)
Jakarta (26)
Johannesburg (.....)
Buenos Aires (.....)
Sydney (26)
Christchurch (26)
Mawson (.....)

Listen to a weather forecaster talking about the missing temperatures. Write in the temperatures. Then check your answers with a partner.

2 What's it like in your town?   vocabulary; conversation

Put these words in the appropriate place:

cool   cold   hot

freezing .... chilly .... warm .... boiling hot

1   2   3   4   5   6

Label the weather drawings. Use these words:

> changeable   humid   snowy   stormy   wet   windy

Choose words to complete these sentences:

1. What's the weather like today? It's ....
2. What's summer like in your town? It's ....
3. What's autumn like in your town? It's ....
4. What's spring like in your town? It's ....

Compare with others.

3   Winter? What winter?   [listening; discussion]

Look at the temperatures in Exercise 1 again. What do you think? What is winter like in Anchorage, Sydney or Jakarta? Talk about it in groups.

◨◨ ◨◨ Listen to three people talking about winter in these countries. Make notes in the boxes.

What's winter like in …

Anchorage?	*Sydney?*	*Jakarta?*
....	....	....
....	....	....
....	....	....

Check your answers with others. What kind of winter do you prefer?

4   In Scotland, the weather's changeable   [writing]

Write a short description of summer in your town or country.

Summer in my country is ....
Sometimes .... At other times
.... I always ....

In Scotland, the weather in summer is very changeable. Sometimes it's lovely – very sunny and warm. At other times it's really wet and windy. I always take an umbrella when I go out.

QC Now do the **Quick Check** exercises your teacher will give you.

B

1 My ideal day   vocabulary and conversation

Imagine that you can choose the weather you want. Choose the weather for these days.

An ideal day on a winter holiday   An ideal day for a picnic
An ideal day on a summer holiday   An ideal day for a wedding
An ideal day at work   An ideal day for watching TV

Compare your choices with a partner.

2 What do you do when it's very hot?   question forms with *when*; speaking

What do you do when the weather's not ideal? Take it in turns to ask a partner these questions. Think of one more question to ask.

A
1. What do you do when the weather's very hot?
2. What do you do when it's very wet?
3. What do you do when ....?

B
1. What do you do when the weather's very cold?
2. What do you do when the air's very polluted?
3. What do you do when ....?

3 Don't forget the sunscreen!   reading

Look at these expressions. Underline the ones you don't know.

> UVR   sunscreen   sunburn   a shirt with long sleeves
> a hat with a wide brim   sunglasses   shade

Read the text on page 139. Use the information to complete three sentences of advice.

When you're out in the sun, make sure you ...
When you're out in the sun, don't forget ... (*or* don't forget to ...)
When you're out in the sun, remember ... (*or* remember to ...)

THE DANGER HOURS:

On a clear day, around 60% of all UVR for that day comes in the four hours around noon. (11 am to 3 pm). Scattered or thin cloud has almost no effect on UVR levels, and temperature does not affect the amount of UVR.

THE DANGER MONTHS:

UVR levels in South Australia are very dangerous for 6 to 8 months of the year: they can cause sunburn in a short period of time. The most dangerous months are November to February.

- Many surfaces reflect a lot of UVR – for example snow, sand, white paint and water. Fresh snow reflects back almost 90% of the UVR that falls on it. When you are out in the sun:

- use a strong sunscreen – 15+.
- wear a shirt with long sleeves.
- wear a hat with a wide brim and keep it on.

- wear sunglasses that keep out most of the UVR.
- cover your skin between 11 am and 3 pm.

- when it is possible, change your plans – don't go out into the sun between 11 am and 3 pm.
- keep in the shade from trees, buildings, and umbrellas when you are outside.

Prepare a role play. Choose Situation 1 or 2.

Situation 1
A: It's your first day in a hot country. You want to enjoy the sun. Tell your friend where you are going and what you plan to do. Reply to your friend's comments.
B: You are a bit worried about your friend. It's a hot sunny day. Give some advice.

Situation 2
A: It's your first day in a cold country. You want to go skiing because it's a sunny day. Tell your friend where you are going and what you plan to do. Reply to your friend's comments.
B: You are a bit worried about your friend, who doesn't know the dangers of sunshine on snow. Give some advice.

QC Now do the **Quick Check** exercises your teacher will give you.

C

1 Natural disasters   discussion

A earthquake

B hurricane

C flood

D bush fire

Look at these photos. Can you name the country in each photo? Work with a partner.

Check your guesses with the teacher.

2 We quite often get earthquakes [vocabulary]

How often do you get these in your area? Put ticks in this table.

	never	not very often	sometimes	quite often	very often
storms	......	......	......	......	......
gales or hurricanes (very strong winds)	......	......	......	......	......
floods	......	......	......	......	......
bush or forest fires	......	......	......	......	......
earthquakes	......	......	......	......	......

Compare your answers with a partner.

3 What do you do if there's a storm? [If constructions with present simple]

Ask two people these questions:

– What do you do if there's a storm?
– How do you feel?

Report their answers.

Example: *If there's a storm, Jon goes out and watches it because he enjoys the excitement, but Timo is frightened: he stays in.*

Is there anyone in your class who knows the answer to these questions?

– What's the best thing to do if there's an earthquake?
– What's the best thing to do if there are floods?
– What's the best thing to do if there are gales?
– What's the best thing to do if there are fires?

4 If you hear the fire bell [writing with *if* clauses]

Imagine that you are staying in a hotel. With a partner, discuss the best thing to do in these situations:

– You hear the fire bell.
– You go out of the room and see smoke in the corridor.
– You're on the tenth floor.
– You run outside and realise you've left your passport in your room.
– Your room is next to the lift.

Write fire instructions in English to go on a hotel door. Begin each one with *If*.

Example: *If you hear the fire bell leave the building immediately.*

QC Now do the **Quick Check** exercises your teacher will give you.

PERSONAL STUDY WORKBOOK

- pronunciation work
- reading about protection against the weather
- *What's it like ...?*
- writing notes for guests
- visual dictionary – climate

REVIEW OF UNIT 20

1 I often apologise   vocabulary; conversation

In what situations do you apologise most often? Talk about your answers with a partner.

Example: *I often apologise to my manager for being late.*

2 I'm sorry I'm late   making apologies

Prepare an apology for
the following situations.
1. You were late for class.
2. You left your book at home.
3. You were away all last week.
4. You didn't do the set homework.

Change partners and try out your apologies on each other.

▭ Listen to four English people. Match each apology with a situation: 1, 2, 3 or 4.
Would apologies in your first language be different from the ones on the recording?

REVIEW OF UNIT 21

1 People don't really need cars   need / don't need + noun

What do people really need? Choose three things from the picture and convince a
partner. (If you don't think people need any of these things, suggest other things.)

112570

2 Children need to feel secure   need / don't need + infinitive; discussion

Are needs different for children and adults? Look at this list of things which
psychologists say children need. Put a tick if you think adults also need these things.

Children need	Adults need
to have enough food and drink	......
to be warm enough	......
to be close to another person	......
to have someone who loves them	......
to feel secure	......
to learn about the world	......

Talk about your ideas with others. Can you add to the list for children and for adults?

23

CELEBRATIONS

Language focus:
offering, inviting
accepting, declining
shall for offers

Vocabulary:
national festivals, family celebrations

A

1 National festivals   vocabulary; discussion

In which country do people celebrate in this way?
What are they celebrating?

Which festivals or celebrations are the most important
in your country? List them in order.

1. ....
2. ....
3. ....

Compare your choices and talk about the festivals in groups.

– What are your reasons for putting them 1, 2, 3?
– Are the festivals traditional (very old, haven't changed for many years) – or are they modern
  or new ones?
– What happens on the festivals? (Do people light candles? give gifts? have feasts?)
– Are the festivals commercialised? Are they changing?

142   Unit 23 CELEBRATIONS

2 Kwanzaa

Look at these questions. With the help of the pictures, can you answer any of them?

– What is Kwanzaa?
– When is it?
– Where do people celebrate Kwanzaa?
– Why do people celebrate it?
– What do people do during Kwanzaa?

Now read this magazine article about Kwanzaa. As you read, take notes to answer the questions.

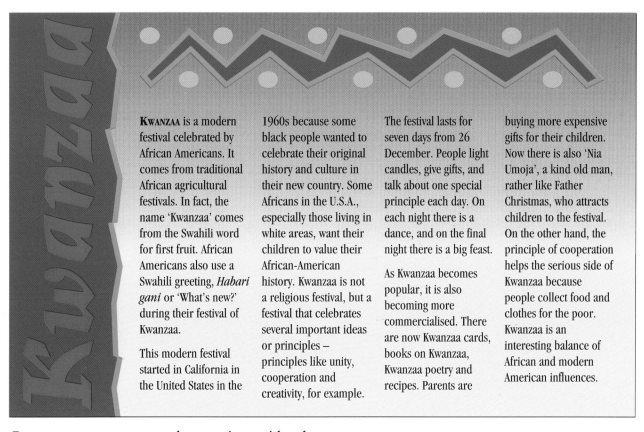

KWANZAA is a modern festival celebrated by African Americans. It comes from traditional African agricultural festivals. In fact, the name 'Kwanzaa' comes from the Swahili word for first fruit. African Americans also use a Swahili greeting, *Habari gani* or 'What's new?' during their festival of Kwanzaa.

This modern festival started in California in the United States in the 1960s because some black people wanted to celebrate their original history and culture in their new country. Some Africans in the U.S.A., especially those living in white areas, want their children to value their African-American history. Kwanzaa is not a religious festival, but a festival that celebrates several important ideas or principles – principles like unity, cooperation and creativity, for example.

The festival lasts for seven days from 26 December. People light candles, give gifts, and talk about one special principle each day. On each night there is a dance, and on the final night there is a big feast.

As Kwanzaa becomes popular, it is also becoming more commercialised. There are now Kwanzaa cards, books on Kwanzaa, Kwanzaa poetry and recipes. Parents are buying more expensive gifts for their children. Now there is also 'Nia Umoja', a kind old man, rather like Father Christmas, who attracts children to the festival. On the other hand, the principle of cooperation helps the serious side of Kwanzaa because people collect food and clothes for the poor. Kwanzaa is an interesting balance of African and modern American influences.

Compare your answers to the questions with others.

Which of these is the most suitable title for each paragraph? Choose a, b or c.

Paragraph 1:
a. Greetings
b. Swahili expressions
c. What does Kwanzaa mean?

Paragraph 2:
a. African–American history
b. Features of Kwanzaa
c. Principles of Kwanzaa

Paragraph 3:
a. Gifts for Kwanzaa
b. Cooperation and commercialism
c. Adults and children at Kwanzaa

Talk about Kwanzaa.

– What do you think about Kwanzaa?
– Do you like the idea of creating a new festival?
– Is Kwanzaa similar to festivals in your country?

3 In the old days, people sang writing

Write a short article or a poem about festivals and celebrations. Choose a celebration or festival and say what you think about it. You can use the ideas in the boxes to help you if you like.

> One of the most popular festivals (celebrations) in .... is
> ....
>
> It has changed in number of ways. In the old days (Traditionally), people danced and sang (or ....), but now they watch the celebrations on the television (or ....).
> The celebration is much more fun now, because you can .... (or because people ....).
> In my opinion, the festival is now too commercialised (or old fashioned or ....).

> FIESTA
>
> **F**ull of fun
> **I**nterest too
> **E**nd of winter
> **S**kies are blue
> **T**ime to dance
> **A**ll night through.

QC Now do the **Quick Check** exercises your teacher will give you.

B

1 Would you like to come? vocabulary; discussion; inviting

Do you usually celebrate birthdays or name days? Talk about what you do.

What happened on your last birthday or name day? Tell a partner.

Think of a place you like in your town (a restaurant, club, disco, hotel – or your own home). You want to invite some English friends there for your birthday celebration. You phone one of them. What do you say in English?

With a partner, complete this telephone conversation. What words can you use to make the invitation?

JENNY: Hello.

YOU: Hello, it's .... here. Is that Jenny?

JENNY: Oh, hi. Yes, it is. How are things?

YOU: Fine, thanks. How about you?

JENNY: Oh, fine. Things are a bit busy at work at the moment ...

YOU: Really? Look, it's my birthday on Saturday.

JENNY: Oh, Happy Birthday!

YOU: Thank you. I'm having a party at .... (add a place). .... (add an invitation question).

Read your phone conversation to another pair.

CD Listen to the start of this phone conversation. Write down the invitation question. Is yours similar?

2 Saying yes   `accepting invitations; listening`

CD Listen as the conversation goes on. How does the friend accept the invitation?
Write down her words.

Now practise a similar telephone conversation with a partner. Invite your partner to a
celebration. Take turns to be the English friend.

3 Saying no   `declining invitations`

What reasons do you give when you can't go to parties, dinners, or other celebrations?
Add reasons to this list. Which reasons are appropriate ones in your society?

I'm too busy.   I'm not feeling well.   I've got to stay in and look after the children.
I've got to go to bed early because I'm going on a long trip tomorrow.
I'm going to another party on the same night.

Talk about your ideas with others. Which invitations do you never decline in your
country? Why? Compare with others.

CD Listen to a second telephone conversation. What reason does the friend give?
Listen and write it down.

He can't come because ....

Check your answer with others.

Go around the room. Take it in turns to be A or B.

A: Invite different people to a celebration.
B: Accept or decline, but remember to give a reason.

QC Now do the **Quick Check** exercises your teacher will give you.

C

1 Shall I do the washing up?   *shall* for offers

Look at these questions. They are all ways of
offering help. Match each one with a picture.

A. Shall I set the table?
B. Shall I get you a cup of tea?
C. Shall I take the dog out for a walk?
D. Shall I do the washing up?
E. Shall I get you a newspaper?

CD Listen to five conversations – people are offering help. Match each with an offer
(A to E). Say if the other person accepts the offer (says *yes*). Number 1 is an example.

Conversation 1: Offer .*B*.....   Does the other person accept? .*Yes*....
Conversation 2: Offer ....   Does the other person accept? ....
Conversation 3: Offer ....   Does the other person accept? ....
Conversation 4: Offer ....   Does the other person accept? ....
Conversation 5: Offer ....   Does the other person accept? ....

2 Yes, that would be wonderful! | accepting or declining offers |

With a partner, choose two situations. Take it in turns to be the guest and the host.

Situation 1
A: Offer to make a drink for a friend who is tired.
B: Accept or decline the drink.

Situation 2
A: A colleague invites you for dinner. After the meal, offer to do the washing up.
B: Accept or decline the offer.

Situation 3
A: A friend invites you for lunch. Before the meal, offer to set the table.
B: Accept or decline the offer.

Situation 4
A: A friend invites you for dinner. When you get to the friend's house, the friend is really tired and the meal is not cooked. Offer to cook the meal.
B: Accept or decline the offer.

3 Anyone who comes to your home is a guest | listening and discussion |

Listen to two people, one from St Lucia in the West Indies and one from India, talking about hospitality in their countries. Complete the notes.

Speaker 1:
The best thing about being a host in St Lucia is that you can:
– show everybody where to go.
– .... the best ....
– .... the best ....
– ....

Speaker 2:
One of the best things about Indian culture is the hospitality .... Anyone who comes to your home is .... they are comfortable and give them something to .... You should offer them something, even just ....

Check your answers with others.

Write a paragraph similar to your notes. Choose one of these beginnings.

1. The best thing about being a host in my country (or .... – another country) is that you can ....

2. One of the best things about my culture (or .... – another culture) is the hospitality. Anyone who comes to a home ....

QC Now do the **Quick Check** exercises your teacher will give you.

PERSONAL STUDY WORKBOOK

* invitations and offers
* reading about Spanish festivals, including La Tomatina – a tomato throwing festival
* listening to dialogues of invitations and reasons for declining
* writing replies to invitations
* visual dictionary – celebrations

REVIEW OF UNIT 21

1   I want to spend, spend, spend | pronunciation: initial consonant clusters |

Listen and repeat.

Listen to the sentences and tick the sound you hear at the beginning of the last word.

/bl/	/br/	/pl/	/pr/		/bl/	/br/	/pl/	/pr/
1.	......	......	......	3.	......	......	......
2.	......	......	......	4.	......	......	......

Listen to the example. Give similar responses to *smile, sleep, snore* and *stop*.

Example: You hear: *spend*   You say: *I want to spend, spend, spend.*

2   I really want to play | consonant clusters and sentence rhythm |

Fill in the missing words. Two of them are *friend* and *space*. Guess the others.

I've got a guitar and I really want to play.
I've got a nice flat and I really want to ....

I've moved to the city and I really love the place;
I've got a big garden and I really need the ....

I'm going on a holiday, I'm travelling to Spain;
I don't want to drive, so I'm going on the ....

I've got lots of money and I really want to spend.
But I'm all on my own and I really need a ....

I'm out in the evenings and I dance till I drop;
I love modern music and I don't want to ....

Do you like lots of fun? Do you like a happy style?
Then forget all your troubles and ...., ..., ...!

Listen and check your answers. Say the sentences with a partner.

REVIEW OF UNIT 22

1   What was your first holiday like? | speaking: *was like* |

Study the examples.

What was the weather like yesterday? It was wet.
What was your first teacher like? She was terrible!

In pairs, choose from the list. Take turns to ask
and answer questions.

> your first trip to another country
> your first day at work or at university
> your first driving lesson
> your first holiday
> your first English lesson

2   Wise words for the fridge | writing advice |

Design a mini-poster with words of advice to put on a fridge door. Choose one of
these beginnings. Then have a poster display. Read your posters out to others.

If you want to learn English ...   If you want to live to be a hundred ...
If you want to be a perfect partner ...   If you want people to like you ...
If you want to be rich ...

24

LOOKING AHEAD

Language focus:
the present simple for talking about the future
the future simple for future facts and predictions

Vocabulary:
age and attitudes to age
personal predictions about the future
predictions about the future of the world

A

1 Thirty-five will be a good age | future simple tense for future facts |

Choose an age you'd like to be in the future and write it down. Think of two good things about being that age. Work in groups. Ask each other questions.

Examples: A: *When will you be thirty-five?*
B: *I'll be thirty-five in five years from now.*
A: *Why do you think thirty-five will be a good age?*
B: *Because I'll have a better job and I'll travel a lot.*
My children will be at school and I'll have more time.

Think again of the age you chose and complete each of these sentences:

At the age of (............)

1. I want to be (a) .... (job/career)

2. I'd like to live in .... (place)

3. I hope to have (a) .... (things)

4. I want to (do) .... (activity)

5. I'd like to be a (more) .... (er) person. (personality)

Talk about your sentences with two others. Ask for reasons behind their choices.

Example: A: *I want to be a manager in my company.*
B: *Why?*
A: *Because I want to change the company and make it international. What about you?*

2 I'll need to travel a lot

I'll need to / I'll have to

Two people wrote about what they want for the future. Match the beginnings of the sentences with appropriate endings.

1. Well I'd like to be a doctor, so …
2. I want to live in Tanzania, so …
3. I'd like to speak it when I get there, so …
4. I hope to be a famous writer, so …
5. I'd like to get my degree in literature as well, so …
6. I want to get some good ideas for my stories, so …

a. I'll have to take the entrance exams for medical school next year.
b. I'll need to write a very popular book.
c. I'll need to travel a lot and see different cultures.
d. I'll need to learn Swahili.
e. I'll need to work hard at university.
f. I'll probably need to go to language classes in the evening.

Look again at your answers to Exercise 1. Are there things you will need to do to make your hopes come true? Tell others what you will need to do.

3 Is age important?

reading and discussion

When do you think these stages of life begin and end? Write in appropriate numbers.

| baby | child | youth | young adult | middle age | old age |

0 – ……… ……… – ……… ……… – ……… ……… – ……… ……… – ……… ……… – ?

Discuss your opinions in groups.

Do people worry about getting older in your country?
How about you? Compare your views.

Read this letter to an English newspaper.

Dear Sir,
I'd like to make a comment about the programmes and advertisements we see on TV: there are no positive images of old people at all. Young people on TV have a lot of money, good jobs and wonderful clothes. They travel in fast cars or planes and have exciting lifestyles. But what about the old people we see in programmes or ads? They live alone, they are usually poor, they never go anywhere, they never do anything. I think the people who make programmes should be more careful. Is that really what our society thinks of older people? Is that really what our young people can hope for in the future? Remember we'll all be old one day – if we're lucky!
Yours faithfully,

Do you agree with the writer of the letter? Do you think attitudes to older people are the same on TV in your country?

QC Now do the **Quick Check** exercises your teacher will give you.

1 You'll never get a good job!

| reading and writing predictions; discussion |

Read these predictions from the past. Check any difficult words in your dictionary. Underline the simple future verbs.

When I was younger …
– my teachers said, 'You'll never get a good job, you're too lazy!'
– my mother said, 'You'll have a good life, because you try hard and you work hard.'
– my father said, 'You won't keep a cent in your pocket, you're so stupid with money.'
– my best friend at school once said, 'You'll be an important person one day, I'm absolutely sure!'
– my first manager said, 'You just won't make a good sales assistant. You'll never be confident enough.'

Has anyone ever made a prediction about you? Complete one or two of these sentences.

My mother (*or* father) said, 'You'll (*or* you won't) ....'

My teacher(s) said, 'You'll (*or* you won't) ....'

.... said, 'You'll (*or* you won't) ....'

Compare your sentences and talk about them. Were the predictions right? Were they wrong?

2 I read my stars in the paper

| vocabulary and discussion |

Compare your reactions to the picture and talk about it. Have you ever used any of these ways of predicting the future? Do you think it is possible to predict a person's future?

3 You'll have two sons
listening and discussion

▭ Listen to this true story about a fortune teller at a fairground. As you listen, note down four of the fortune teller's predictions.

The fortune teller said:
1. You'll ....
2. You'll ....
3. You'll ....
4. You'll ....

Check your notes with a partner. Have you heard any other stories about predicting the future?

4 Your English will soon be very good
writing predictions

Imagine you are a fortune teller. Think of some other people in your class. Write two predictions about them.

Examples: *You'll marry a tall, dark, handsome stranger. (Bilge)*
You won't be a rich person but you'll be very happy. (Jens)

Read out your predictions to the class. Can the others guess who you have written about? Do they agree with the prediction?

QC Now do the **Quick Check** exercises your teacher will give you.

C

1 I think children will need languages
the future simple; discussion and listening

What things will children need in the future to be happy and successful? Complete the sentence. Choose at least two expressions from the box, or use your own ideas.

In the future, children will need:

....

to spend more time at school   to speak more languages   to read a lot
to learn more about other countries   to know how to use computers
to learn more about business   to have lots of imagination   to be very fit
to enjoy their hobbies   to learn to be patient   to tackle the problem of pollution

▭ ▭ Listen to four speakers talking about what children will need in the future. Tick seven things in the box that the speakers mention. One speaker says they'll need something that is not in the box.

What is it? ....

2 What will happen to our world?

Read the article. Do you agree with the predictions? Tick to show your opinion.

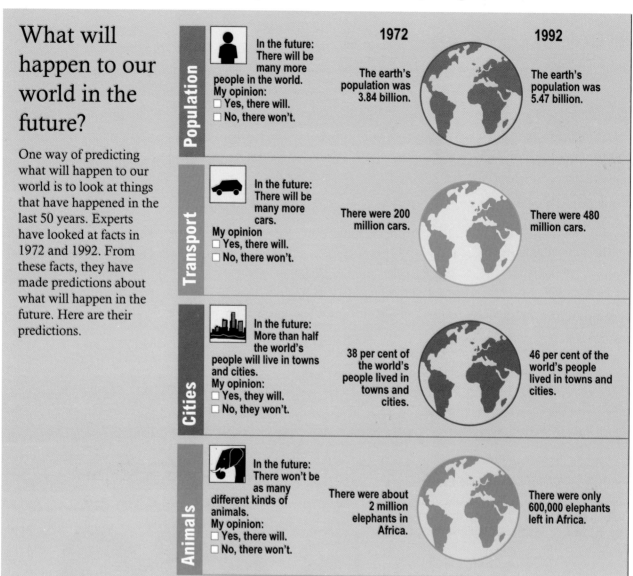

What will happen to our world in the future?

One way of predicting what will happen to our world is to look at things that have happened in the last 50 years. Experts have looked at facts in 1972 and 1992. From these facts, they have made predictions about what will happen in the future. Here are their predictions.

Population

In the future:
There will be many more people in the world.
My opinion:
☐ Yes, there will.
☐ No, there won't.

1972
The earth's population was 3.84 billion.

1992
The earth's population was 5.47 billion.

Transport

In the future:
There will be many more cars.
My opinion
☐ Yes, there will.
☐ No, there won't.

There were 200 million cars.

There were 480 million cars.

Cities

In the future:
More than half the world's people will live in towns and cities.
My opinion:
☐ Yes, they will.
☐ No, they won't.

38 per cent of the world's people lived in towns and cities.

46 per cent of the world's people lived in towns and cities.

Animals

In the future:
There won't be as many different kinds of animals.
My opinion:
☐ Yes, there will.
☐ No, there won't.

There were about 2 million elephants in Africa.

There were only 600,000 elephants left in Africa.

Work with a partner. Compare your choices. Try to think of reasons for them.

Example: A: *The article says there will be many more people in the world.*
B: *Yes, I think there will, because people will have more children.*
A: *I don't agree. I've ticked* No, there won't, *because people won't want more children, and small families will be possible.*

What else will change? Will the world have more countries or fewer?

QC Now do the **Quick Check** exercises your teacher will give you.

PERSONAL STUDY WORKBOOK

- pronunciation practice of /l/ and /r/
- a reading text about being single and being a couple
- *will* forms
- writing notes for a friend before you go out
- reflecting on your future learning plans
- visual dictionary – society

REVIEW OF UNIT 22

1 When I have a free day writing; speaking

Choose three of the six sentences and complete them in three different ways. Use some of these expressions.

eat a lot   sing a song   listen to the radio   feed the cat   talk to a friend
have a drink   lie in bed and think   do exercises   do nothing
read a newspaper   drink lots of water   watch TV   phone my mother or father
take aspirin   play with the children   go out with friends   write in my diary
work very hard   see the doctor   have a shower   read my mail
put a note on the wall   go to a film   stay at home   have a nice meal
go on a holiday   buy some new clothes   write a letter   sleep a lot

1. When I get home after work, …
2. When I have a free day, …
3. When I'm bored, …
4. When I haven't got any money, …
5. When I go on a long journey, …
6. When it's really hot, …

Read your sentences to two others, and find out if they do the same things.

Example: A: *When I get home after work I read the newspaper. Is that what you do?*
  B: *No, I never read the newspaper in the evening. When I get home, I feed the cat and play with the children. What about you, Chris?*
  C: *Well, I have a drink and watch TV.*

REVIEW OF UNIT 23

1 Please come and see my new flat discussion; inviting and accepting or declining

In your country, do people do any of these things when someone moves into a new flat or house? Tell a partner.

Take gifts (What gifts are appropriate?)   Send cards   Have a party (What kind of party?)

Do you have a special word in your language for this kind of celebration? In English-speaking countries, the word is a *housewarming*.

CD Listen to a person asking three friends to a housewarming party. Which is correct?

1. Two of the friends can come to the party, one can't.
2. One friend can come, two can't.
3. One friend can come, one can't, one doesn't want to.
4. One friend can come, one isn't sure, one can't come.

What excuse does the woman give?

2 Enjoy your new flat! reading; writing

You want to send a card to a friend who has just moved into a new house or flat.
Write a short message to go inside the card.

Good luck in your new home!

GRAMMAR REFERENCE

The verb *to be* (present simple) Subject pronouns

LONG FORM		SHORT FORM	
POSITIVE	NEGATIVE	POSITIVE	NEGATIVE
I am	I am not	I'm	I'm not
You are	You are not	You're	You aren't (*or* You're not)
She/he is	She/he is not	She's/he's	She/he isn't (*or* She's/he's not)
It is	It is not	It's	It isn't (*or* It's not)
We are	We are not	We're	We aren't (*or* We're not)
They are	They are not	They're	They aren't (*or* They're not)

Note:

You = one person *or* more than one.

Example:

Are you a doctor? *Are you doctors?*

There is; there are

To describe or list things, use *there is* (1 thing) or *there are* (2 or more things).

LONG FORM		SHORT FORM	
POSITIVE	NEGATIVE	POSITIVE	NEGATIVE
There **is**	There **is not**	There**'s**	There **isn't**
There **are**	There **are not**	There **are**	There **aren't**

Question forms with *there is, there are*

*Is **there** ...?*
*Are **there** ...?*
*What is **there** ...?*

Examples:
Is there a phone? (Yes, there is.)
Are there any public phones? (No, there aren't.)
What is there in the room? (There's a phone.)
Where is the phone? (It's in the room.)

The verb *to be* – question forms and short answers

Are you ...?	Yes, I am. No, I'm not.
Is she or he ...?	Yes, he is. No, she isn't.
Is it ...?	Yes, it is. No, it isn't.
Are we ...? (Are you ...?)	Yes, we are. No, we aren't.
Are they ...?	Yes, they are. No, they aren't.
What's (What is) your job?	I'm a student.
What's their job?	They're mechanics.
What is it?	It's a chair.
What are they?	They're computers.
Where are you?	I'm in the building.
Where is it?	It's on the table.
Where are they?	They're on the first floor.
How many computers are there?	There's (there is) one. There are two, three, lots.

A and *an*

Use *a* before consonants.
Use *an* before vowels: **a**, **e**, **i**, **o** and **u**.

Note:
Use *a* before the vowel **u** when it has the sound /juː/ (as in *university*).

Examples:
a secretary a parent a doctor a plumber a mechanic
*an **a**ccountant an **e**xit an **i**nteresting person an **o**pen door an **u**nemployed person*
*a **u**niversity*

Saying where things are

1. in   on   by   beside   next to   under   over

*The computer is **in** the room, **on** the table, **beside** the book (or **next to** the book).*
*The table is **by** the window and **over** the bin.*
*The bin is **under** the table.*

2. opposite   at the end of   on the first floor
   along the corridor   on the left (on the right)
   one floor up (one floor down)

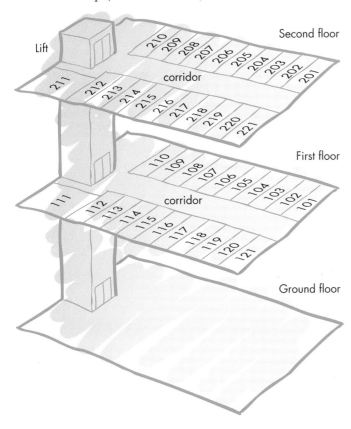

*The lift is **at the end of** the corridor.*
*Room 101 is **on the first floor, along the corridor, opposite***
  Room 121.
*Room 201 is **one floor up.***

Word order in sentences

Adjectives usually come before the noun.

Examples:
an important job
a good life

Subjects usually come before the verb.
***Petra** (subject) is (verb) a nurse.*
***They** (subject) are (verb) doctors.*

Any – see Unit 3.

2

Have got (present simple)

LONG FORM	NEGATIVE	SHORT FORM	NEGATIVE
I have got	I have not got	I've got	I haven't got
You have got	You have not got	You've got	You haven't got
She has got	She has not got	She's got	She hasn't got
He has got	He has not got	He's got	He hasn't got

Subject pronouns

Note:
Always use a subject. Use a subject noun or a subject pronoun.

Examples:
***I**'ve got a brother.*
   (Not: ~~have got a brother, got a brother.~~)
***Pedro**'s got (has got) a son.*
   (Not: ~~got a son~~)
= ***He**'s got a son.*
   (Not: ~~got a son~~)
***Julia**'s got (has got) a son.*
   (Not: ~~has got a son~~)
= ***She**'s got a son.*
   (Not: ~~got a son~~)
***Pedro and Julia** have got a son = **They**'ve got a son.*

Connecting words – and/but

Use ***and*** to connect two things that are grammatically similar.

Examples:
Two nouns: *a son and a daughter; Pedro and Julia*
Two clauses: *She's got a son and they've got a daughter.*

With more than two things, use *and* only before the last one:

I've got a mother, a father, a brother and four cousins.

Use **but** when there is a contrast.

Examples:
In my country, April is sunny but cold.
We've got a daughter but we haven't got a son.

Possessive adjectives

I – my	you – your	he – his	she – her
it – its	we – our	they – their	

Note:
The possessive adjective agrees with the possessor.
If the possessor is a man (Pedro/he) – use *his*.
If the possessor is a woman (Julia/she) – use *her*.

Examples:
Pedro's got a son. **His** *son's eight years old.*
Pedro's got two daughters. **His** *daughters are nine and seven.*
Julia's got a son. **Her** *son's eight years old.*
Julia's got two daughters. **Her** *daughters are nine and seven.*

Genitive 's (or possessive 's)

For nouns, add *'s* to a singular noun or *'* to a plural noun. (Irregular nouns add *'s*.)

Examples:
my wife's mother (= the mother of my wife)
my parents' house (= the house of my parents)
my children's teacher (= the teacher of my children)
Pedro's son (= the son of Pedro)
Charles's daughter (= the daughter of Charles)

Note:
's has different meanings:
– it shows possession
– it is the contraction of a verb (for example, *is* or *has*)

Examples:
my wife's mother (= the mother of my wife)
My wife's in India. (= My wife **is** *in India.)*
Pedro's son (= the son of Pedro)
Pedro's got a son. (= Pedro **has** *got a son.)*

Question forms and answers

> **Have** *you* **got** *...? Yes, I have. No, I haven't.*
> **Has** *he/she/it* **got** *...? Yes, he has. No, she hasn't.*
> **What have** *you* **got**? *I've got a pen. I haven't got a book.*
> **Short form: What've you got?**
> **What has** *it* **got**? *It's got a kitchen. It hasn't got a bath.*
> **Short form: What's it got?**
> **How many have** *you* **got**? *I've got one, two, three, lots.*
> *I haven't got any.*
> **How many has** *she* **got**? *She's got one. He hasn't got any.*

Plurals of nouns

For most nouns, add **s**.

one son	two son**s**	one daughter	four daughter**s**
one mother	two mother**s**	one father	three father**s**

For nouns ending in *y*, change *y* to **ies.**

one family	three famil**ies**	one country	five countr**ies**

Some nouns have irregular plurals.

one child	two child**ren**	one wife	two wi**ves**
one man	two m**en**	one life	two li**ves**
one woman	two wom**en**		

A, some and *any* – see Unit 3.

3

Have (present simple) used for food, drink and meals

POSITIVE FORM	NEGATIVE FORM
I have	I don't have (do not have)
You have	You don't have (do not have)
She/he has	She/he doesn't have (does not have)

Examples:
I **have** *breakfast at eight, but my sister* **has** *her breakfast at nine.*
I always **have** *coffee and I* **don't have** *anything to eat.*
My sister **has** *some bread and cheese, and a glass of milk. She* **doesn't have** *a hot drink for breakfast.*

Present simple question forms – with the subject *you*

See also Unit 5.

Do you **have** ...?	Do you have coffee for breakfast?
What **do** you **have** ...?	What do you have for breakfast?
What time **do** you **have** ...?	What time do you have breakfast?
What **do** you **do**?	I'm an engineer.
What **do** you **think**?	I think question forms are easy!

Would you like ...? and I'd like ...

To ask for things or to order things politely, use:
I'd like …
To find out what other people want, use:
Would you like …?

QUESTION FORMS	ANSWER FORMS
What would you like?	I'd like some coffee. (I would like) He'd like tea. (He would like) She'd like a roll. (She would like)
Would you like tea or coffee?	I'd like tea, please. Or: Tea, please.
What time would you like breakfast?	I'd like it at seven. Or: Seven.

I'd like for wishes – see Unit 6.

Countable and uncountable nouns

When the focus of use is on separate things that can be counted, the nouns are called *countable nouns*. They can be singular or plural.

Example:
one cup, two cups, three cups, some cups

When the focus of use is not on separate things that can be counted but on a general amount or quality, the nouns are called *uncountable nouns*. They are never plural.

Example:
rice, tea, coffee, water
I've got tea or coffee.
I'd like some rice, please.

Note:
Some nouns can have both countable and uncountable meanings or uses.

1. Some uncountable nouns become countable when they mean *a kind of* or *a category of*.

Example:
a sugar (= not sugar in general, but one of several different chemicals called sugars)
a China tea (= not tea in general, but one of the different kinds of tea made in China)

2. Some uncountable nouns are used like countable nouns when they mean a portion (or a unit) of something.

Example:
People ask for: *Three coffees, please* or *I'd like two sugars in my tea.*
This is a short way of saying: *Three **cups** of coffee, please* or *I'd like two **spoonfuls** of sugar* (or *two sugar **cubes***) *in my tea.*

A, some and any (with countable and uncountable nouns)

Use *a* in questions and positive or negative statements with singular nouns.
Use *any* in questions and negative statements with plural nouns and uncountable nouns.
Use *some* in positive statements with plural nouns and uncountable nouns.

	Questions	+ state- ments	– state- ments
With singular nouns:	a	a	a
With plural nouns:	any	some	any
With uncountable nouns:	any	some	any

Examples:

Questions	Statements
Have you got *a* pen?	I've got *a* pen. I haven't got *a* pen. (*1 pen* = singular noun)
Have you got *any* pens?	I've got *some* pens. I haven't got *any* pens. (*2 or more pens* = plural noun)
Have you got *any* money?	I've got *some* money. I haven't got *any* money. (*money* is an uncountable noun)

How much and How many ...?

Use *How many …?* to ask the number of countable nouns.

Examples:
How many cups of tea would you like? Three.
How many teas would you like? (= cups of tea) *Three.*
How many chairs are there in the room? Ten.

Use *How much …?* for uncountable nouns.

Examples:
How much rice would you like? One kilo.
How much cereal would you like? Two kilos, please.

Connecting words – or

Use *or* to connect possible choices.

Examples:
Would you like coffee or tea?
To be or not to be – that is the question.

Asking the price

To ask the price of something, use:
How much is …? (for one thing, or for an uncountable noun.)
How much are …? (for more than one thing – plural countable nouns.)

Examples:
How much is rice? $3 a kilo. (£, francs, DM, etc.)
How much are bananas? £2 a kilo.
How much is this cheese?
How much is that coffee?
How much are these pens?
How much are those calculators?

This and *that, these* and *those*

How much is this?

How much is that?

How much are these?

How much are those?

Use **this** and **that** for a singular noun, or an uncountable noun.
Use **this** for things close to you. Use **that** for things that are not so close.
Use **these** and **those** for a plural noun.
Use **these** for things close to you. Use **those** for things that are not so close.

Present simple question forms – 3rd person verb forms

	Do	I	buy clothes?
Where	**do**	you	buy clothes?
Why	**do**	we	buy clothes?
How often	**do**	they	buy clothes?
	Does	he/she	buy clothes?
Where	**does**	he/she	buy clothes?
Why	**does**	he/she	buy clothes?
How often	**does**	he/she	buy clothes?

Present simple verbs – 3rd person forms

I	**buy** my clothes.	He	**buys** his clothes.
You	**buy** your clothes.	She	**buys** her clothes.
We	**buy** our clothes.		
They	**buy** their clothes.		

Giving reasons – *because*

When speaking, people often begin an answer with *because* to give reasons or explanations, after the question *Why?*
In written English, and also in spoken English, *because* comes in the middle of a sentence: it introduces a reason or explanation for something in the first part of the sentence.

Examples:
Why do you buy socks from the market?
Because they're cheap.
I buy my socks from the market, because they're cheap.

Adjectives of colour

Adjectives of colour come before the noun, like other adjectives.

Example:
A red rose; a blue jacket.

Prepositions of place – *Where do you buy …?*

Where do you buy clothes, food, etc.?

At (or from) the market.   In (or from) a shop.
At/from the supermarket.   In/from a small shop (a boutique).
At/from Harrod's   In/from a shop called Harrod's.
(the name of the shop, usually followed by *'s*)

The present simple – when is it used?

Use the present simple to talk about permanent situations or habits, routines and customs. In Unit 5 the focus is on habits, routines and customs.
(For the present simple in permanent situations, see Unit 11.)

Examples:
I get up quickly at five in the mornings. (routine)
She always has a good breakfast. (routine)
I eat little snacks all day. (habit)
In Britain, people stand in queues to wait for the bus.
  (custom)
In Egypt, men kiss on both cheeks. (custom)

The present simple – negative forms

POSITIVE	NEGATIVE
I sing in the bathroom.	I **don't** sing in the bathroom. (do not)
You listen to me.	You **don't** listen to me.
He reads a newspaper.	He **doesn't read** a newspaper.
She has a good breakfast.	She **doesn't have** a good breakfast.
We go downstairs.	We **don't** go downstairs.
They shake hands.	They **don't** shake hands.

Questions with the present simple

Most verbs use the auxiliary *do* to form questions.

Examples:

	Do *you smoke at work?*
What	**do** *they do on Sundays?*
Where	**do** *I go shopping?*
Why	**do** *we eat between meals?*
	Does *she smoke at work?*
What	**does** *he do on Sundays?*
Where	**does** *she go shopping?*
Why	**does** *he eat between meals?*

Short answers
Do you smoke at work? Yes, I do. No, I don't.
Does she smoke at work? Yes, she does. No, she doesn't.

Note:
The verb *to be* is different. It does not use the auxiliary *do* for questions.

POSITIVE SENTENCE	QUESTION FORM
I'm (I am) a nurse.	*Am I a nurse?*
You're (you are) a morning person.	*Are you a morning person?*
He's (he is) a teacher.	*Is he a teacher?*
We're (we are) mechanics.	*Are we mechanics?*
They're (they are) secretaries.	*Are they secretaries?*

Adverbs of frequency

To talk about how often something happens, use an adverb of frequency.

Example:
How often do you go shopping?

100% 90%	80% 70%	60% 50%	40%	30% 20%	10% 0%
always	usually	often	a lot	sometimes	never

Expressions of frequency		
Once a day	twice a day	three, four (etc.) times a day
Once a week	twice a week	three, four (etc.) times a week
Once a month	twice a month	three, four (etc.) times a month
Once a year	twice a year	three, four (etc.) times a year

Expressions of time

To talk about when something happens, use an expression of time.

Example:
When do you go shopping?
– *First thing in the morning.*
– *In the morning.*
– *In the afternoon.*
– *In the evening.*
– *All day.*
– *At the weekend.*

Expressing opinions

To say your opinions, use *I think …* or the verbs *seem* or *look*.

Examples:
I think (that) curly hair is nice.
I think (that) your brother is a practical person.
Your brother seems a practical person.
He looks a bit sad.

Responding to opinions

1. Expressing interest – *Really? That's interesting.*

Examples:
A: *For me, it's important for a friend to be a non-smoker.*
B: *Really?*

C: *Sev plays golf on Saturday.*
D: *That's interesting. Where does he play?*

2. Agreeing – *Me too. I think so too. I agree.*

Examples:
A: *I think curly hair is nice.*
B: *Me too.* (or *I think so too. / I agree.*)

3. Disagreeing – *Do you think so? I don't think so, really* at the end of a contradictory statement.

Examples:
A: *I think she's very confident.*
B: *Do you think so? (or I don't think so. / I disagree. or No, she's shy, really.)*

Modifiers

a bit   quite   very

Examples:
They're a bit selfish.
He's quite shy.
She's very serious.

I'd like for wishes

Use *I'd like* to talk about wishes that are possible *or* impossible.
I'd like a good job. (possible)
I'd like to be a baby again. (impossible)

Too and not enough

Too big	not small enough
Too small	not big enough

Examples:
His hair's too long.   *His hair's not short enough.*
                          ~~His hair's not enough short.~~

7

Can (present simple) – forms

SUBJECT	POSITIVE	NEGATIVE (SHORT FORM)	NEGATIVE (LONG FORM)
I You She He We They	can cook.	can't cook.	cannot cook.

Can is the same with all subjects. It is usually followed by a verb (in the infinitive form, without *to*). In short answers, it can be used without the following verb.

QUESTION FORMS	SHORT ANSWERS – POSITIVE AND NEGATIVE
Can you cook?	Yes, I can. No, I can't.
Can he/she cook?	Yes, he can. No, she can't.

Can – uses

Use *can* to talk about:

1. ability or skill

Example:
Derva can play the piano.

2. permission

Example:
You can buy cigarettes at 16 in my country.

Use *can* (simple present) or *could* (simple past of *can*) for

3. requests.

Example:
Can you get me a glass of water?
Could you write it on the board, please?

The past simple of can – forms and uses

SUBJECT	POSITIVE	NEGATIVE (SHORT FORM)	NEGATIVE (LONG FORM)
I You She He We They	could cook.	couldn't cook.	could not cook.

Could is the past of *can*. Like *can*, it is the same for all subjects. The verb which follows *can* or *could* does not change.

POSITIVE	NEGATIVE	QUESTION FORM
I could	I couldn't (I could not)	Could I/you/he ...?

Use *could* for:

1. talking about abilities, skills, or permission in the past.

Examples:
When I was a child, I could run all day. (past ability/skill)
Could you read when you were three? No, I couldn't read, but I could sing. (past ability/skill)
I couldn't go to school yesterday, I was ill. (past ability)
When my grandmother was young, women couldn't vote, and they couldn't go to university. (past permission – here lack of permission)

2. requests in the present (slightly more polite than *can*).

Examples:
Could you pass the bread, please?
Could I try the suit on, please?

Anybody and anywhere

Use *anybody* to talk about any person at all – unspecified.

Example:
Anybody can remember telephone numbers.

Use *anywhere* to talk about any place at all – unspecified.

Example:
My sister can read anywhere – in a noisy room, in a crowded train, in a car, anywhere!

For *anything* and *anyone*, see Unit 12.

The past simple tense of *to be* – positive and negative forms

PRESENT SIMPLE		PAST SIMPLE	
POSITIVE	NEGATIVE	POSITIVE	NEGATIVE
I'm (I am)	I'm not (I am not)	I was	I wasn't (I was not)
You're (You are)	You're not (You are not)	You were	You weren't (You were not)
She's (She is)	She isn't (She is not)	She was	She wasn't (She was not)
He's (He is)	He isn't (He is not)	He was	He wasn't (He was not)
We're (We are)	We aren't (We are not)	We were	We weren't (We were not)
They're (They are)	They aren't (They are not)	They were	They weren't (They were not)

Question forms – *to be*, present simple and past simple

PRESENT SIMPLE	PAST SIMPLE
Am I?	Was I?
Are you/we/they?	Were you/we/they?
Is she/he?	Was she/he?

The past simple of *to have* and *to go* in positive sentences

I/You/She/He/We/They had
I/You/She/He/We/They went

For the question forms of *to have*, *to go* and other verbs, see Unit 8. For the negative forms, see Unit 9.

Talking about what you like or don't like

To say what you like or don't like, use the verb + a noun, or the verb + an *-ing* form.

Examples:
I like my flat.	*I don't like my flat.*
I like the shops.	*I don't like the shops.*
She/He likes people.	*She/He doesn't like people.*
I like living in my flat.	*I don't like living in my flat.*
I like going to the shops.	*I don't like going to the shops.*
She/He likes working with people.	*She/He doesn't like working with people.*

Note:
The structure *I like/don't like + -ing* is often used in British English. In the United States (and sometimes in Britain) people say: *I like to shop*; *I like to have a party*.

To say how much you like or don't like something, use:

I quite like	I like	I love	I really love
I don't really like	I don't like	I hate	I really hate

Using *a* and *the*

With singular nouns:

*I like **a** park.*   *I like **the** park near my flat.*

Use *a* when you mean any park or a park in general.
Use *the* when you mean one particular park (not parks in general).

With plural nouns:

I like parks.   *I like **the** parks near my flat.*
*I like **some** parks.*

Don't use *a* or *the* when you mean all parks, or parks in general.
Use *some* when you mean some but not all parks.
Use *the* when you mean some particular parks (not some others), e.g. the parks near my flat (but not the parks in the centre of town).

Past tense question forms with *did*

PRESENT TENSE	PAST TENSE
Do you like cats?	**Did** you like cats?
When **do** you like cats?	When **did** you like cats?
Why **do** you like cats?	Why **did** you like cats?
What **do** you like about cats?	What **did** you like about cats?
What **don't** you like about cats?	What **didn't** you like about cats?

PRESENT TENSE	PAST TENSE
Does she like cats?	**Did** she like cats?
When **does** he like cats?	When **did** he like cats?
Why **does** she like cats?	Why **did** she like cats?
What **does** he like about cats?	What **did** he like about cats?
What **doesn't** he like about cats?	What **didn't** he like about cats?

Note:
The question forms for most verbs follow this pattern. The verb *to be* and *can* have different question forms for the present simple and for the past simple tenses.

9

Past simple tense – when is it used?

Use the past simple tense for actions or events completed in the past. It is often used with time expressions such as *yesterday*, *last week*, *last month*, *two years ago*, etc.

Past simple tense (regular verbs) – positive statements

PRESENT		PAST	
I/you/we/they	move.	I/you/we/they	mov**ed**.
She/he	moves.	She/he	mov**ed**.
I/you/we/they	miss.	I/you/we/they	miss**ed**.
She/he	misses.	She/he	miss**ed**.
I/you/we/they	stay.	I/you/we/they	stay**ed**.
She/he	stays.	She/he	stay**ed**.

Past simple tense – negative statements

I/you/he/she/we/they	**didn't** move.
	(long form = **did not** move)
	didn't miss. (**did not** miss)
	didn't stay. (**did not** stay)

Note:
To be and *can* are different.

Object pronouns

Ada phoned me.	(I received a phone call from Ada.)
Ada phoned you.	(You received a phone call from Ada.)
Ada phoned her.	(She received a phone call from Ada.)
Ada phoned him.	(He received a phone call from Ada.)
Ada phoned us.	(We received a phone call from Ada.)
Ada phoned them.	(They received a phone call from Ada.)

Connecting words – sequence in time

First, I went shopping.

Then, I went home.

After that, I went to the theatre.

10

See the irregular verb table on page 174.

Note:
I was born is an unusual form. Learn it as a set expression.

Examples:
I was born in 1925.
They were born in Istanbul.
My cousin and I were born in the same year.

11

The present continuous tense

POSITIVE STATEMENTS	NEGATIVE STATEMENTS
I'm learning.	I'm not learning.
(I am learning.)	(I am not learning.)
You're learning.	You aren't learning.
(You are learning.)	(*or* You're not learning. = You are not learning.)
He's learning.	He isn't learning
(He is learning.)	(*or* He's not learning. = He is not learning.)
She's learning.	She isn't learning.
(She is learning.)	(*or* She's not learning. = She is not learning.)
We're learning.	We aren't learning.
(We are learning.)	(*or* We're not learning. = We are not learning.)
They're learning.	They aren't learning.
(They are learning.)	(*or* They 're not learning. = They are not learning.)

The present continuous tense – when is it used?

Use the present continuous tense for:
– things that are happening now

Example:
What are you doing in there? I'm reading a book.

– temporary situations

Example:
I'm staying in a hotel this week.

– developing situations

Example:
The cost of living is going up in our country.

For the present continuous used for future events, see Unit 12.

Time expressions – *at the moment, today, just now*

These time expressions are often used with the present continuous. They emphasise that things are happening now.

Just, with the present continuous, is similar in meaning to *only* – it emphasises that the action is happening now and is not long lasting.

Example:
What are you doing in there? I'm just making a cup of tea.
= *I'm only making a cup of tea.* (an action that is not long lasting)

Connecting expressions – *so is/are, as well, also*

These expressions connect additional similar statements. Note their position in the sentence:

*Pollution is going up, and unemployment is **also** going up.*
*Pollution is going up, and unemployment is going up **also**.*
*Pollution is going up. **Also**, unemployment is going up.*

*Pollution is going up. Unemployment is going up, **as well**.*
*Pollution is going up. **So is** unemployment.*
*Pollution is going up and **so is** unemployment. (And **so are** prices.)*

Agreement of subject and verb

When the subject is an expression (with *of*), the first noun (head noun) is the one that the verb agrees with.

Example:
*The **number** of years **is** going up.*
*The **popularity** of sports **is** staying the same.*
*The **price** of cigarettes **is** going up.*
*The **hours** of sunshine **are** important for plants.*

12

The present continuous and *going to* + infinitive for future events – how are they used?

Use the present continuous for future events that are already arranged.

Example:
The manager is seeing Mrs Smith at 10:30 on Thursday.
(At the moment of speaking, the event is still in the future, but already arranged.)

Going to + infinitive is another way of talking about future events. Its use is quite similar to the present continuous form and many native speakers use either one or the other.

Example:
The manager is seeing Mrs Smith next week.
or
The manager is going to see Mrs Smith next week.

Going to + infinitive is often preferred to express a strong intention or determination to do something in the future.

Example:
I'm certainly going to complain to the manager about this hotel room.
(Here, the future event is not exactly arranged, but the speaker has a strong intention to carry it out.)

Note:
It's easy to confuse the present continuous of the verb *to go* and the *going to* + infinitive form.

He's going to a party on Saturday.
(This is the present continuous of the verb *to go* – it indicates an event in the future, already arranged.)
He's going to study English in New Zealand.
(This is the *going to* + infinitive form, and indicates intention.)

Going to + infinitive – forms

Positive statements

I'm going to study. (I am going …)
You're going to study. (You are going …)
He's going to study. (He is going …)
She's going to study. (She is going …)
We're going to study. (We are going …)
They're going to study. (They are going …)

Negative statements

I'm not going to study.
You aren't going to study. (*or* You're not going to study.)
She or he isn't going to study. (*or* He's not going to study, She's not going to study.)
We aren't going to study. (*or* We're not going to study.)
They aren't going to study. (*or* They're not going to study.)

Question forms

	Are you going to study?		Is he going to study?
What	are we going to study?	What	is she going to study?
When	are they going to study?	When	is he going to study?
Why	are you going to study?	Why	is she going to study?

Anyone and anything

Use *anyone* to talk about any person. It is often used in questions. Notice its position in the question form.

Example:
*Is **anyone** coming to visit you this month?*

Use *anything* to talk about unspecified things. Notice the position of *anything* or *anywhere* in the question form.

Examples:
*Are you doing **anything** in January?*
*Are you going **anywhere** in the summer?*

13

Comparatives and superlative adjectives

There are three main groups of comparative/superlative adjectives.

Group 1
For group 1, add a suffix (*er/est*):

1. If the word ends in *e*, add *r/st* to the adjective:

ADJECTIVE	COMPARATIVE ADJECTIVE	SUPERLATIVE ADJECTIVE
nice	nicer	the nicest
fine	finer	the finest

2. Add *er* and *est* to the adjective:

ADJECTIVE	COMPARATIVE ADJECTIVE	SUPERLATIVE ADJECTIVE
green	greener	the greenest
poor	poorer	the poorest

3. Double the final consonant letter of the adjective and add *er* and *est*:

ADJECTIVE	COMPARATIVE ADJECTIVE	SUPERLATIVE ADJECTIVE
big	bigger	the biggest
wet	wetter	the wettest

4. Change *y* at the end of the adjective to *i* and add *er* and *est*:

ADJECTIVE	COMPARATIVE ADJECTIVE	SUPERLATIVE ADJECTIVE
easy	easier	the easiest
lively	livelier	the liveliest

Group 2
Some adjectives have a different form for the comparative and the superlative adjectives:

Different forms – *good/bad*:

ADJECTIVE	COMPARATIVE ADJECTIVE	SUPERLATIVE ADJECTIVE
good	better	the best
bad	worse	the worst

Group 3

For group 3, add a word in front of the adjective *more* (comparative) or *most* (superlative). For the opposite, use *less* (comparative) or *least* (superlative).

1. Add *more* and *most* to most adjectives with three or more syllables, and to some with two syllables:

ADJECTIVE	COMPARATIVE ADJECTIVE	SUPERLATIVE ADJECTIVE
interesting	more interesting	the most interesting
interesting	less interesting	the least interesting
exciting	more exciting	the most exciting
exciting	less exciting	the least exciting
modern	more modern	the most modern
modern	less modern	the least modern

2. Adjectives ending in *ied*, *id*, or *ing*, add *more* and *most* to the adjective:

ADJECTIVE	COMPARATIVE ADJECTIVE	SUPERLATIVE ADJECTIVE
varied	more varied	the most varied
varied	less varied	the least varied
boring	more boring	the most boring
boring	less boring	the least boring
splendid	more splendid	the most splendid
splendid	less splendid	the least splendid

Comparatives and superlative adjectives – how are they used?

They are used for comparing things, people, or qualities.

cheaper
Cup A is cheaper than cup B.

The comparative form – comparing two separate people or things

cheapest
Cup A is the cheapest.

The superlative form – comparing three or more separate people or things

Note:
The comparative form – comparing one separate thing with a group

the others

Cup A is cheaper than the others.
(cheaper than the ones in the other group)

Negative forms – *not as ... as*

In negative sentences, use *not as* (+ the adjective) *as* ...

My brother is not as tall as me.
    (= *My brother is shorter than me.*)
My car is not as big as your car.
    (= *My car is smaller than your car.*)
Towns are not as good as cities.
    (= *Cities are better than towns.*)

Question forms

Are you taller than your brother?
Are you as tall as your brother?
Is your car bigger than my car?
Are cities better than towns?
*Which is **the** cheapest café in town?*
*Which is **the** most modern city in the world?*

Note:
Remember to use *the* when using the superlative adjective form. Don't use *the* with comparative adjectives.
Often the superlative is followed by the preposition *in*.

*I am **the** tallest in my family.*
*My car is **the** biggest in the world.*
*This is **the** most interesting unit in the book.*
    (Note also *This unit is **the** most interesting in the book.*)
*My town is **the** best in the country.*

Comparative adjectives and modifiers

a bit smaller, a lot smaller, much smaller, much, much smaller

Examples:

My car

This car is a bit smaller than my car.

My car

This car is much smaller / a lot smaller than my car.

Both

Use *both* for two things that share a similar quality or feature.

Examples:
Are both London and Tokyo crowded?
  (= *Is London crowded and is Tokyo crowded?*)
Yes, both cities are very crowded.

14

The present perfect tense

For the present perfect tense, use *have* or *has* + the past participle.

Positive statements

LONG FORM	SHORT FORM
I have tried.	I've tried.
You have tried.	You've tried.
He/She has tried.	He's/She's tried.
We/They have tried.	We've/They've tried.

Negative statements

LONG FORM	SHORT FORM
I have not tried.	I haven't tried. (*or* I've not tried.)
You have not tried.	You haven't tried (*or* You've not tried.)
He/She has not tried.	He/She hasn't tried. (*or* He's/She's not tried.)
We/They have not tried.	We/They haven't tried. (*or* We've/They've not tried.)

Question forms

Have I tried? Have you tried? Have we tried?
Have they tried?
Has she tried? Has he tried?

The present perfect tense – how is it used?

Use the present perfect tense:

1. to talk about actions or situations which happened at any unspecified time, up to now.
Ever and *never* are often used to express this.

Examples:
Have you ever tried motor racing? (= Have you tried it at any time in your life, up until now?)
No, I've never tried it. (= at no time in my life, up until now)
I've tried it once. (= in my life, at an unspecified time – and until now, once only)

2. to talk about actions or situations which happened within a defined time period that is not yet finished. Time expressions which refer to a period *up to now* (*this year, this week, this month, in modern times*, etc.) are often used to express this.

Examples:
Have you had a cold this year? (= Have you had a cold at any time at all within this year and up to and including now? It's not yet the end of the year.)

For the present perfect with *just* and *yet*, see Unit 16.

The present perfect/simple past

Compare:
1.
*Have you ever watched motor racing? Oh, **I've watched** it a lot.*
(= Many different times in my life, up until now – the times are unspecified)
2.
*Have you ever watched motor racing? Yes, **I watched** it on TV yesterday afternoon.*
(= the time is specified – the action happened yesterday, in a time that is now finished)

Always use the simple past with time expressions that refer to a past time that is now finished, for example, *yesterday, last week, last year, at five o'clock yesterday, in 1968*, etc.

Yesterday I watched soccer on TV.
(Not: *Yesterday I've watched soccer on TV.*)

Note:
Some verbs have past participles that are different from simple past tense forms:

	SIMPLE PAST	PRESENT PERFECT
to go	I went.	I have gone.
to be	I was.	I have been.
to do	He did.	He has done.

15

-ing forms

-ing forms are used in the object position after a verb; with *for* and with *before* and *after*.
They are also used as the subject of a sentence (in this use they are sometimes called gerunds).
They are used to form the present continuous tense after the verb *to be* (in this use they are sometimes called participles). See Units 11 and 12.

-ing forms are constructed by adding *-ing* to the infinitive form of a verb, as in:
to keep	keeping
to see	seeing
to go	going

GRAMMAR REFERENCE

For some verbs, remember to:
1. double the last letter:
to forget   forge**tt**ing
to put   pu**tt**ing
2. remove the final *e*:
to us**e**   using
to los**e**   losing
3. change the last letter:
to li**e**   **ly**ing

Examples of use:
-ing forms in the subject position:
***Writing** is my favourite activity.*
***Writing information down** helps me to remember it.*

-ing forms in the object position:
*I like **eating**.*
*I keep **forgetting** things.*

-ing forms with *for*:
Computers are useful for storing information.
Diaries are handy for remembering dates.

-ing forms with *before* and *after*:
Before going home, I always tidy my desk.

Notes:
1. In English, *before going home = before I go home*. You can say either *before going home* or *before I go home*.
2. *Before -ing* (or *after -ing*) can go in the first part of the sentence, or in the second part:
I always tidy my desk before going home.
After drinking your coffee, you always put away your cup.
You always put away your cup after drinking your coffee.

-ing forms in questions

Do you keep forgetting things?
Do you wash up after drinking your coffee?
Is a dictionary useful for learning words?
Is using a computer a good thing?

16

Relative pronouns – how are they used?

who   that   where   when   which

A relative pronoun is used after a noun to add a clause which gives more information about that noun.
Compare:
We saw the man. (= we don't say anything about the man)
We saw the man who works in the shop. (= we give some more information about the man)

The relative pronoun joins two clauses together.

Example:
We saw the man. He works in the shop.
We saw the man who works in the shop. (The two clauses are now one sentence.)

who is used for people. (*The woman who ...; the child who ...*)
that is used for things. (*The maps that the groups drew ...*)
It can sometimes be used for people or places. (*The doctor that works in the medical centre ...; I like the restaurant that has Indian food ...*)
where is used after a place. (*The university where they work ...*)

Present perfect with *yet*

This is another example of the present perfect tense used to talk about actions or situations at any unspecified time, up to now.
Yet emphasises that the action is expected.

Examples:
Have you met your new neighbours yet? (The speaker expects the meeting at some time around now.)
I haven't seen them yet. (= I expect to see them, but it hasn't happened up to now.)

Present perfect with *just*

Just is used with the present perfect to talk about very recent events.

Example:
My neighbours have just moved in. (= It happened very recently.)

When we use *just*, the time period is unspecified, but it's always not very long ago.

The train's just left! (= I can see it, but I can't get on it.)
They've just moved into a new house. (= They moved at some unspecified time – not very long ago.)

Giving directions

Imperatives
People often use the imperative form (*go, turn, take, drive, cross*) when giving directions.
For the imperative, use the verb in the infinitive form, without *to*.

Examples:
(to go)   *Go down the street.*
(to turn)   *Turn right at the traffic lights.*
(to take)   *Take the third street after the roundabout.*

Expressions of place or direction
Examples:
*It's **on the left**.*
*It's **on the right**.*
*Go **down** the street.*
*Go **up** the street.*
*Go **past** the lights.*
*Go **along** this street.*
*Go **straight ahead**.*
*Turn **left at** the car park.*
*Cross **at** the traffic lights.*

17

Adjectives and adverbs

Uses
Adjectives say what someone or something is or seems like. They often go with a noun (*a **nice** day*) or complete a sentence after *is*, or *seems*. (*She seems **nice**.*)
Adverbs are used to give more information about an action and often go after a verb to tell us how, when or where, the action happened. (*She eats **quickly**. She's coming **soon**. He sat **there**.*)

Form of adverbs
Some adverbs are formed by adding *-ly* to the adjective (*nice – nicely; quick – quickly*)

Note:
Some adjectives end in *-ly* and cannot be adverbs (*lively, friendly, lovely*).

Position
Many adverbs go in the middle, or at the end of a clause. Some can also go at the beginning.

Examples:
***Quickly**, he opened the door.*
*He **quickly** opened the door.*
*He opened the door **quickly**.*

Many adjectives go
– with (often before) a noun:
a nice day.
– after verbs like *be*, *seem* and *look*:
It seems interesting.

Connecting words of sequence

To show the order of events in a sequence, use connecting words like *first, then, next, after that*, etc.

Example:
*To make a cup of tea, **first** boil the water. **Then** warm the tea pot. **Next**, put in the tea. **After that**, pour in the water. Wait five minutes. **Then** pour it into the cup and drink it.*

18

Should and shouldn't

Positive statements
I, you, she, he, it, we, they should + infinitive without *to*

Examples:
*Travellers should **drink** a lot of water.*
*You should **have** a sleep after a flight.*

Note:
Don't use *to* after *should*.

Negative statements
I, you, she, he, it, we, they shouldn't (*should not*) + infinitive

Examples:
A tourist shouldn't be too loud.
Passengers shouldn't put their bags under the seat.

Questions
Should I, she, he, it, you, we, they + (infinitive without *to*)?
(The speaker wants to know the other person's opinion.)

Example:
Should tourists take travellers' cheques?

Should + infinitive and shouldn't + infinitive – how are they used?

Use *should* + infinitive to say that it's a good idea to do something (your personal opinion), or to talk about actions that are recommended.
Use *shouldn't* + infinitive to say that it's not a good idea to do something (your personal opinion), or to talk about actions that are not recommended.

Have to / don't have to

Positive statements
I, you, we, they have to + infinitive (without *to*)

Examples:
You have to get a visa when you arrive in Turkey.
Travellers have to have two photos for their visa.

She, he, it has to + infinitive (without *to*)

Example:
She has to get a new passport.

Negative statements
I, you, we, they don't have to + infinitive (without *to*)

Example:
I don't have to have a passport to go to Germany, because I'm a member of the EEC.

She, he, it doesn't have to + infinitive (without *to*)

Example:
She doesn't have to fill in a landing card, because she's a member of the EEC.

Questions
Do I, you, we, they have to + infinitive (without *to*)?

Example:
Do I have to have a passport to go to Australia?

Does she, he, it have to + infinitive (without *to*)?

Example:
Does he have to have a passport to go to Venezuela?

Note:
It is **not** appropriate to use the forms:
I, you, we, they haven't to …
She, he, it hasn't to …
Have I, you, we, they to …?
Has she, he, it to …?

Have to / has to

Have to and *has to* are used to talk about actions that are necessary or required – the obligation comes from a rule, a law, or another person.
Don't have to / doesn't have to are used to talk about actions or events that are not required or obligatory.

Somebody and someone

Somebody/someone = a person (unspecified)

Examples:
A good tourist is someone who enjoys the local food.
A good tourist is somebody who respects the local traditions.

19

Would like (+ noun or + infinitive with *to*)

POSITIVE STATEMENTS	
LONG FORM	SHORT FORM
I would like	I'd like
You would like	You'd like
She/He/It would like	She'd/He'd/It'd like + noun *or* + infinitive
We would like	We'd like
They would like	They'd like

In spoken English the short form is often used.

NEGATIVE STATEMENTS	
LONG FORM	SHORT FORM
I would not like	I wouldn't like
You would not like	You wouldn't like + noun *or* + infinitive
She/He/It would not like	She/He/It wouldn't like
We would not like	We wouldn't like
They would not like	They wouldn't like

Questions
Would I, you, she, he, it, we, they like (+ noun or + infinitive)?

Notes:
For questions, use the long form only.
For short positive answers, use the long form only.

Examples:
Would you like to come?
Yes, I would. (Not: *Yes, I'd.*)

Would like

Would like ('d like) is used to talk about things, situations or events you wish for, that are possible or impossible.

Would ('d) like + noun
Examples:
I'd like a new car.
I'd like more free time.
I'd like more free time to read.

Would ('d) like + infinitive (with *to*)
Examples:
He'd like to be an actor. (possible)
She'd like to be a cat. (impossible at the moment)
They'd like to live happily.
They'd like to live to be 100 years old.

Would with other verbs
Would ('d) can be used with other verbs, to talk about situations or events that are hypothetical or imagined. It is always followed by the infinitive of the verb, without *to*:

Examples:
I'd be sick.
I'd keep forgetting.
I wouldn't like to be 100 years old, because I'd be sick and I'd keep forgetting things.
I'd know a lot. People would listen.
I'd like to be 100 years old, because I'd know a lot, and people would listen to me.

Connecting expressions – *on the one hand, on the other hand*

These expressions link sentences that express a contrast. They are often used in writing.

Examples:
I'd like to be 100 years old. On the one hand, I'd be sick, but on the other hand, I'd know a lot and people would listen to me.
I wouldn't like to be 100 years old. I'd know a lot, of course, but on the other hand I'd be sick and I wouldn't like that.

Note:
On the other hand can be used without *on the one hand*, provided that the sentence expresses a contrast of meaning.

20

Apologising

Uses
The uses of apologies are different in different cultures and they also vary from person to person; but generally we apologise when we accept that something is our fault.
For example:
– when we cause an accident
– when we bump into someone
– when we don't keep appointments
– when we give a negative answer
– when we realise that we have given wrong
   information, etc.

Spoken forms

Spoken or informal:
Sorry.
I'm sorry.
You can add other words to make the apology more polite:
I'm so/terribly/very/extremely/ever so sorry.

More formal:
I apologise.
The company regrets that …

Note:
Often the speaker will offer an excuse, a reason or an explanation at the same time as the apology, as in:
I'm sorry I knocked over your cup, I didn't see it.
I'm ever so sorry, I forgot all about our appointment.
I'm terribly sorry I didn't phone, but I was busy all day.

The choice of words and the intonation of an apology (or a complaint) both influence the degree of politeness.

Written forms

– informal notes to friends or peers; often the same forms as spoken English are used:

I'm sorry I can't come but …

– formal letters of apology
– in response to invitations:

I regret that I am unable to attend …
I very much regret that I am unable to attend.

– accepting responsibility:

We apologise for the noise in the street next to the hotel.
I apologise (sincerely) for not replying to you sooner.

Complaints

In English, when making a complaint, it is polite to start with:
Excuse me … or *Pardon me*, or *I'm sorry, but …*

Examples:
Excuse me, but I'd like to complain about this watch.
I'm sorry, but this doesn't fit.

21

need (+ noun or + infinitive) / want (+ noun or + infinitive)

Positive statements

I, you, we, they need (+ noun or + infinitive with *to*)
I, you, we, they want (+ noun or + infinitive with *to*)
He, she needs (+ noun or + infinitive with *to*)
He, she wants (+ noun or + infinitive with *to*)

Negative statements

I, you, we, they don't need/want (+ noun or + infinitive with *to*)
She, he doesn't need/want (+ noun or + infinitive with *to*)

Note:
Sometimes people use the negative form *needn't* (*need not*) as in, for example:
You needn't stay in place of *You don't need to stay.*
In this case, the infinitive is used without *to*.

Questions

Do I, you, we, they need/want (+ nouns or + infinitive)?
Does she, he need/want (+ nouns or + infinitive)?

Need and want – how are they used?

Need

Use *need* to talk about something that the speaker considers necessary, important or useful (but is not always required by law, or by an outside rule).

Examples:
I need a pen, my only other pen is broken. (= The speaker considers it necessary.)
You need to go to university to get a good job. (= The speaker considers it important, but it is not required by law.)

Want

Use *want* to talk about a thing or an action that the speaker desires, or wishes to do or have.

Examples:
I want a new pen; I have several, but I like new things.
(The speaker wishes to have it but doesn't need it because he/she already has pens.)
They want to live in New Zealand.
(They don't need to live in New Zealand, they like the idea.)

22

What's it like? questions – forms

What's it like? (*What is it like?*)

Example:
What's winter like in Adelaide? It's not very cold.

What's she like? (*What is she like?*)

Example:
What's your new manager like? (*What's she like?*)
She's quite lively.

What are they like?

Example:
What are the cities like? (*What are they like?*)
They're quite polluted.

What's it like? questions – how are they used?

Use *What's it like?* questions to ask for a general description of a person, a thing, or a place and to ask for someone's opinion of a person, a thing, or a place.

Examples:
What's John like?
He's tall, with dark hair. He's really nice.
What's your computer like?
It's great. I love it.

Note:
In spoken English, *What is she like?/ What is he like?* can easily be confused with *What does she or he like?*

Example:
What does he like for breakfast?
(In rapid speech, this sounds similar to: ~~What's he like for breakfast?~~)
Answer: *He likes toast and tea.*

What's he like at breakfast?
Answer: *He's very quiet.*

If (clause) + present tense or imperative – form

Positive statements
(*If* + present tense), (present tense for the consequence)

Examples:
If there's a storm, I feel nervous.
(or: *I feel nervous if there's a storm.*)
If she feels nervous, I get unhappy.

(If + present tense), (imperative for advice)

Examples:
If you see smoke in the corridor, shut the door quickly.
(or: *Shut the door quickly if you see smoke in the corridor.*)
If there's a flood, go to the top of the house.

Question forms

Examples:
What's the best thing to do if there's a storm?
(or: *If there's a storm, what's the best thing to do?*)
What do you do if there's a storm?
How do you feel if there's a storm?

When (clause) + present tense or imperative – form

(When + present tense), (present tense for the consequence)
Examples:
When the weather's hot, we sit out in the garden.
(or: *We sit out in the garden when the weather's hot.*)
When you're cold, you put on a heavier coat.

(When + present tense), (imperative for advice)
Examples:
When it's hot, wear a hat.
(or: *Wear a hat when it's hot.*)
When you're in the sun, don't forget your sunscreen.

Questions
Examples:
What do you do when the weather's very hot?
(or: *When the weather's very hot, what do you do?*)
What does he do when the air's polluted?

When and if clauses – how are they used?

They are both used to talk about what happens to things or people in certain circumstances. *When* is usually used to talk about circumstances that are common or frequent. *If* is often used for more unusual circumstances. Compare:
What do you do if there's an earthquake?
(An earthquake is probably an unusual circumstance.)
What do you do when it rains?
(Rain is probably quite common.)
Do people listen when she talks?
(She probably talks quite often.)
Do people listen if she talks?
(She probably doesn't talk very often.)

There is not a great difference in meaning between the two, and the choice of one or the other often depends on the speaker's sense of the circumstances.

23

Inviting, offering – forms

Examples:
Can you (she, he, they, we) come to (my party / London) on Tuesday?
Would you (she, he, they, we) like to come to (my party / London) on Tuesday?

I'm having a party on Tuesday, would you like to come?
I'm going to London on Tuesday, can you come?

Note:
The *would you* form is generally more polite with a person the speaker doesn't know well.

Related forms
Please come to my party on Tuesday.
How about coming to my party on Tuesday?

Accepting an invitation (saying yes to an invitation)
Oh, thanks (for inviting me), I'd love to come.
Yes, I'd love to.
Yes, I'd like that very much.
Yes, I can.
Yes, I think I can.

Saying perhaps to an invitation
I'm not sure, can I call you?
I think I can, but can I call you later?
I think I'm free on Tuesday, can I call you later to confirm?

Declining an invitation (saying no to an invitation)
The speaker often gives a reason or an excuse. The word *no* is quite often omitted.

I'm sorry, but I'm (busy/ not free) on Tuesday.
It's nice of you to invite me, but I'm afraid I'm really busy on Tuesday.
I'd love to come, but I'm afraid I'm going out to dinner on Tuesday.
Thanks for inviting me, but I'm going to Paris on Tuesday.
(No,) I'm afraid I can't, I'm working late on Tuesday.

Offers with *shall* – forms and use

Shall I/we + infinitive without *to*

Examples:
Shall I do the washing up?
Shall we walk the dog for you?

Accepting offers
Yes, please. Thanks a lot.
Yes, I'd love one. (I'd love to.)
Yes, that would be wonderful. (great/nice/lovely)

Declining offers
No, thank you.
No. That's OK.
No, (thank you) I'll do it. (= I shall do it. This is the future simple tense – see Unit 24.)

24

Want, hope, would like – suggesting the future

Some verbs suggest future time when used in the present simple form.

I want a new car. (not immediately but in the future)
I hope to be a doctor one day. (not now but sometime in the future)

The form *I'd like* also has a sense of the future (the future events are sometimes more hypothetical).
I'd like to be rich. (sometime in the future)

Future simple tense – forms

Positive statements short form + *'ll* + *infinitive without* to
I'll you'll she'll he'll it'll we'll they'll …

Examples:
I'll be 30 next year.
They'll be in Japan next month.

Negative statements short form – *won't* + *infinitive without* to
I you he/she/it we they won't …

Examples:
You won't get home before 12.
We won't need cars as much in the future.

Positive and negative statements – *long forms*
I you she/he/it we they will be 30 next year.
I you she/he/it we they will not get home before 12.

Questions – **Will** + *subject* + *infinitive without* **to**
Will I you she/he/it we they …?

Examples:
Will they arrive tonight?
Will she need to take exams?

Notes:
The short form is not used in short answers.

Example:
Will he arrive soon?
Yes, he will. (Not *Yes, he'll.*)

Shall (not *will*) is generally used in the question form when making offers, suggestions or requesting confirmation with *I* or *we*.

Examples:
Shall I do the washing up?
Shall we go out tonight?

The *shall* form is sometimes used in the positive long form with *I* and *we*. The short form removes confusion and is current in spoken English.

Examples:
I shall write to you next week. (I'll write to you next week.)
We shall need to arrive early. (We'll need to arrive early.)

The future simple tense – how is it used?

Use the future simple tense
– to talk about future facts

Example:
I'll be 30 next year.

– to make predictions

Examples:
She'll be president in 2010.
Food will get more expensive.

– to offer to do something in the near future

Examples:
I'll do the washing up.
Shall I do the washing up?

– to talk about arrangements made at the time of speaking

Examples:
I'll see you at nine.
I'll meet you at the restaurant.

Notes:
It is often possible to use *going to* + infinitive instead of the future simple. It often shows strong resolution.

Examples:
You'll be rich one day. (general prediction)
You're going to be rich one day. (more confident prediction)
I'll be the manager of this company one day. (prediction)
I'm going to be the manager of this company! (strong resolution)

The present continuous is usually preferred for arrangements made before the moment of speaking. The future simple is usually preferred for arrangements or decisions made at the time of speaking.

Compare:
We're meeting them in Portugal next month.
(It's already arranged.)
Would you like the fish, or the meat? Erm … I'll have the meat.
(The decision is made at the time of speaking.)

PROJECT

1 Questions to ask

Work in small groups (of about four people). You are planning interviews of the people in your class in order to produce a class yearbook. Write a series of questions. What do you want to find out about other people in your class?

Compare your questions with those of other groups. Make a class list of questions.

2 Interviewing others

Interview one other person in the class. Ask the questions and take notes.

3 Planning the paragraphs

In your groups, plan your paragraphs about the people you interviewed. Get photos of them. Plan each page.

4 Writing the paragraphs

Write your paragraph. Work with a partner. Read each other's work and help each other with the language and the ideas. In your group, look at all your paragraphs and suggest changes to make them better.

5 Adding more general information about the class

Add other information and photos about the class:

- photos and interview with the teacher(s)
- photos of the class in action – if you can, get one of your class to take photos of role plays, line-up activities, poster presentations, etc. You can also write a few sentences to describe these activities.
- photos and short reports of events that happened, parties, excursions, sports events, etc.

Design an attractive cover for the yearbook.

6 Assembling the yearbook

When each group has finished, put your paragraphs together to make a yearbook for your class. Add the pages of general information and photos. If you can, make copies for each person in the class, so that you remember this year!

IRREGULAR VERBS AND PHONETIC SYMBOLS

Irregular verbs

Infinitive	Past simple	Past participle
be	was/were	been
become	became	become
begin	began	begun
bend	bent	bent
bite	bit	bitten
blow	blew	blown
break	broke	broken
bring	brought	brought
build	built	built
buy	bought	bought
can	could	(been able)
catch	caught	caught
choose	chose	chosen
come	came	come
cost	cost	cost
cut	cut	cut
do	did	done
draw	drew	drawn
dream	dreamt	dreamt
drink	drank	drunk
drive	drove	driven
eat	ate	eaten
fall	fell	fallen
feel	felt	felt
fight	fought	fought
find	found	found
fly	flew	flown
forget	forgot	forgotten
get	got	got
give	gave	given
go	went	gone (been)
have	had	had
hear	heard	heard
hit	hit	hit
hold	held	held
hurt	hurt	hurt
keep	kept	kept
know	knew	known
learn	learnt	learnt
leave	left	left
lend	lent	lent
let	let	let
lie	lay	lain
lose	lost	lost
make	made	made
mean	meant	meant
meet	met	met
pay	paid	paid
put	put	put
read /riːd/	read /red/	read /red/
ride	rode	ridden
ring	rang	rung
rise	rose	risen
run	ran	run
say	said	said
see	saw	seen
sell	sold	sold
send	sent	sent
set	set	set
shake	shook	shaken
shine	shone	shone
shoot	shot	shot
show	showed	shown
shut	shut	shut
sing	sang	sung
sit	sat	sat
sleep	slept	slept
speak	spoke	spoken
spell	spelt	spelt
spend	spent	spent
stand	stood	stood
steal	stole	stolen
swim	swam	swum
take	took	taken
teach	taught	taught
tell	told	told
think	thought	thought
throw	threw	thrown
understand	understood	understood
wake	woke	woken
wear	wore	worn
win	won	won
write	wrote	written

Phonetic symbols

Vowels

Symbol	Example
/iː/	see
/i/	happy
/ɪ/	big
/e/	bed
/æ/	sad
/ʌ/	sun
/ɑː/	car
/ɒ/	pot
/ɔː/	taught
/ʊ/	pull
/uː/	boot
/ɜː/	bird
/ə/	among
	produce
/eɪ/	date
/aɪ/	time
/ɔɪ/	boy
/əʊ/	note
/aʊ/	town
/ɪə/	ear
/eə/	there
/ʊə/	tour

Consonants

Symbol	Example
/b/	back
/d/	dog
/ð/	then
/dʒ/	joke
/f/	far
/g/	go
/h/	hot
/j/	young
/k/	key
/l/	learn
/m/	make
/n/	note
/ŋ/	sing
/p/	pan
/r/	ran
/s/	soon
/ʃ/	fish
/t/	top
/tʃ/	chart
/θ/	thin
/v/	view
/w/	went
/z/	zone
/ʒ/	pleasure

Stress
Stress is indicated by a small box above the stressed syllable.
Example: advertisement

ACKNOWLEDGEMENTS

Authors' acknowledgements

We would like to extend warm thanks to Ruth Gairns and Stuart Redman, whose help and support we very much appreciated throughout our work on this shared project.

We are grateful to our readers, whose detailed and constructive comments were extremely valuable to us: Gillian Lazar, Susan Garvin, Virginia Garcia, Diann Gruber, Carol Herrmann, Philip Town, Anthony Nicholson and Antonio Marcelino Campo.

At Cambridge University Press, we would like to express our thanks to our commissioning editor, Peter Donovan, to our editor, Kate Boyce, whose expert guidance and remarkable problem-solving ability smoothed so many difficulties, to James Dingle for his help with the pilot edition, and to the rest of the staff, especially Jeanne McCarten, for their continued support. Our thanks go to Helena Gomm for her editorial skill, patience and good humour, to our design team, and especially Randell Harris, to our recording producers, Peter Taylor and James Richardson, and to the staff at AVP.

Stephen Slater is very grateful both to his colleagues at CALUSA (the Centre for Applied Linguistics in the University of South Australia) for their encouragement and patience, and to all the members of his family in Australia and England who so generously gave up their time to enable him to work on this project.

And finally, a big thank you from Joanne Collie to all the members of her family for their creative ideas and their support.

The authors and publishers would like to thank the following institutions and teachers for their help in testing the material and for the invaluable feedback which they provided:

Insearch Language Centre, UTS, Sydney, Australia; Transfer, Paris, France; Centro Linguistico di Ateneo, Parma University, Parma, Italy; Cambridge Institute of English, Reggio Emilia, Italy; Regency School, Turin, Italy; The Cambridge School, Verona, Italy; Latvia University, Riga, Latvia; Languages International, Auckland, New Zealand; Cambridge English Studies, La Coruña, Spain; Universidad de Navarra, Pamplona, Spain; École d'Ingénieurs, Geneva, Switzerland; Dilko English, Istanbul, Turkey; Chichester School of English, Chichester, UK.

The authors and publishers are grateful to the following copyright holders for permission to reproduce copyright material. While every endeavour has been made, it has not been possible to identify the sources of all material used and in such cases the publishers would welcome information from copyright sources. Apologies are expressed for any omissions.

p. 35: Roger McGough for his poem 'Q' taken from *Melting into the foreground*, published by Penguin. Reprinted by permission of the Peters Fraser & Dunlop Group Ltd; p.47: Wall & Emerson Inc. for extracts from 'Superman' and 'A Cruel Joke' taken from *New Canadian Voices* by Jessie Porter. Reprinted with permission of the publisher Wall & Emerson, Inc. Toronto, Canada; p. 52: *The Guardian* for the extract taken from 'Inside Out'; p. 74: *The Advertiser* for the article 'The Iceman'; p. 83: HarperCollins publishers for the extract on Istanbul taken from *Turkey* by Daniel Farson; p. 91: Gaia Books for the extract taken from *The Book of Massage* © 1984 Gaia Books Ltd, published by Ebury Press; p. 96: *The Guardian* for the extract taken from 'Office workers find method in their morass of paper' 27/8/92; p. 114: HarperCollins publishers for the extract on Turkey taken from *Turkey* by Daniel Farson; p. 121: 'You must have been a beautiful baby' by Robert Mathews, 19/7/92 © *The Telegraph* plc, London 1992; p. 127: *The Advertiser* for the article 'Virago's shorts offended officials'; p. 139: *The Advertiser* for the article 'Beware – skin cancer ...'; p. 152: *The Independent* for the article 'What will happen to our world in the future?' 3/6/92.

The authors and publishers are grateful to the following illustrators and photographic sources:

Illustrators: Veronica Bailey: p. 150; Kathy Baxendale: pp. 6, 7 *b*, 11, 12, 16, 17, 82 *t*, 101, 103 *b*, 119, 155, 158, 159, 161, 162, 165; Peter Byatt: p. 34 *t*; Paul Dickinson: p. 80; David Downton: pp. 25, 26, 90, 104; Nicky Dupays: pp. 14, 149; Richard Eckford: pp. 59, 103 *t*; Max Ellis: p. 40; Philip Emms: pp. 31, 96; Martin Fish: p 79; Spike Gerrell: p. 35; Celia Hart: pp. 6, 8, 81, 85, 123, 136 *t*, 154, 165; Tony Healey: p. 127; Michael Hill: pp. 9, 69, 108 *t*, 136 *b*, 137; Sue Hillward-Harris: pp. 46, 64, 73, 100; Terry Kennett: p. 94; Joanna Kerr: pp. 10, 34 *b*, 65, 66, 82 *b*, 108 *b*, 145; Vicky Lowe: pp. 32, 102; Cathy Morley: pp. 20, 112; Pete Neame: p. 43; Diane Oliver: pp. 7, 47, 98, 144; Giovanna Pearce: pp. 62, 63; Liz Pichon: pp. 39, 106; Tracy Rich: pp. 22, 45, 57, 76, 77, 124; Sunita Singh: pp. 56, 148; Blaise Thompson: p. 118; Emma Whiting: pp. 36, 67, 91; Alison Wisenfeld: p. 130; Celia Witchard: pp. 29, 54, 55, 89.

Photographic sources: Ace Photo Agency: pp. 16 (photo Mauritius), 27 *c* (Thompson), 37 *c* (Nawrocki Stock), 44 *r* (Hince), 51 *tc* (Mauritius), 75 *tl* (Stokes), 88 *bc* (Phototake), 109 (Mauritius) and 137 *l* (Bachmann); Andes Press Agency: p. 66 *cl* (Carlos Reyes); Aviation Picture Library: p. 53 *tl* (Airbus); The Bell Language Schools: p. 86; Bridgeman Art Library: p. 121 (except Naomi Campbell); British Museum: p. 13 *bc* (Gountei Sadahide, *Foreign Families on the Harbour Front at Yokohama*); Britstock IFA: pp. 72 *c*, 83 *t* and *c* (Grafenheim), 88 *br* (Sanders), 119 (Bach) and 132 (Duke); Bubbles Photolibrary: p. 75 *bl* (Thurston); Camera Press: pp. 15 *bl*, 37 *l*, 44 *l* (Horner), 72 *r* (Springer Verlag), 88 *tr* (McDonough) and 141 (flowers); Michael Cole Camerawork: p. 120 *l*; Collections: pp. 141 *br* (Sieveking) and 142 *bc* (Shuel); Comstock: p. 142 *l*; Lupe Cunha: p. 53 *tr*; Gregg Evans International: pp. 15 *c*, 27 *br* (Flowerden), 88 *l* (Ikeda), 114 *cr* (Groves) and 114 *cr* (Patterson); Garden Picture Library: p. 75 *tr* (Legate); Robert Harding Picture Library: pp. 38, 51 *l*, 114 *bl* (Tory), 138 *r* (Helier), 139 *t*, 139 *bcr*, 141 (computer) and 142 *bcr*; Holt Studios International: p. 8 background; Geoff Howard: p. 142 *tc*; Hutchison Library: pp. 136 *l* (Francis) and 139 *bl* (Veritz); Image Bank: pp. 25 *c* (jeans/Hackett), 52 (Brown), 57 (Martin), 72 *l* (Sulle), 75 *br* (Yellow Dog), 80 *l* (Eden/Stockphotos), 80 *c* (Dee), 80 *r* (Novak), 132 *br* (Infocus), 137 *l* (Caufield), 137 *c* (Place), 139 *bcl* (Rankin), 141 (smoking and water) and 151 (Lewin); Frank Lane Picture Agency: pp. 120 *r* (Coppola) and 139 *br* (Hollands); Life File: pp. 15 *tl*, 25 *tl* (tie/Fisher), 44 *cl* (Fisher), 44 *cr* (Thompson), 137 *r* (Lee) and 141 (car and phone); National Gallery of Ireland: p. 13 *tr* (Giambattista Moroni, *Man with Two Daughters*) and *bl* (Patrick Tuohy, *Supper Time*); Next Press Office: p. 25 (except tie and jeans); David Noble: pp. 27 *bcr*, 51 *c*, 136 *r* and 138 *c*; Photo Edit, Tarzana: p. 143 (David Young Wolf (2) and Richard Hutchings); Photolink: p. 124; Powerstock: pp. 27 *bl*, 88 *tc* and 132 *tl*; Rapho: p. 27 *tcr* (Martel); Retna Pictures: pp. 15 *r* (Putland), 37 *r* (Acheson), 121 (Naomi Campbell/Woodward) and 141 (photos and chocolates); Rex Features: pp. 27 *tr*, 35 and 141 (cat, dog, books); The Salvation Army: p. 26; South American Pictures: p. 142 *tr* (Francis); Tate Gallery, London: p. 13 *tl* (David des Granges, *The Saltonstall Family*) and *br* (Michael Andrews, *Melanie and Me Swimming* (courtesy Anthony d'Offay)); Topham/Picturepoint: pp. 51 *r* and 142 *br* (Svenskt Pressfoto).

The photos on pp. 6, 14, 19, 33, 53 *b*, 66 *l*, *cr* and *r*, 95, 114 *l* and *tr*, 131, 141 (light bulb) and 153 were taken by Peter Lake.

t = top, *b* = bottom, *c* = centre, *l* = left, *r* = right

Design and DTP by Newton Harris
Picture research by Marilyn Rawlings

The authors and publishers are grateful to the following for permission to reproduce photographs on the cover:

Image Bank: *l* (Antonio M. Rosario), *tc* (Pete Turner), *c* (Joe van Os) and *tr* inset (Alan Becker); Tony Stone Images: *tr* (Dennis McColeman) and *br* (Peter Correz).